# A FEATHER
# SHORT OF
# FLYING

# A Feather Short Of Flying

# A Feather Short of Flying

By Carl Pohlner, Jr.

A collection of his essays from *The Baltimore Sun*
edited by Professor Andrew Ciofalo
Loyola College in Maryland

Sunspot Books

GALILEO PRESS • BALTIMORE • 1989

*To Sharon, Jen*
*Dan, and Rob*

Published by Galileo Press Ltd.
15201 Wheeler Lane, Sparks, Maryland, 21152

Sunspot Books is the non-fiction imprint of The Galileo Press

Cover Art: Linoleum cut by Carl Pohlner, Jr.
Cover Design: Terri Anne Ciofalo

Publication of this book was made possible
by grants from
The Greater Baltimore Community Foundation,
Noxell Corporation,
Dr. Frank C. Marino Foundation, and
The Morton and Sylvia Macht Foundation.

LIBRARY OF CONGRESS CATALOGING-IN-PUBLICATION DATA

Pohlner, Carl, 1945-
A feather short of flying / by Carl Pohlner, Jr. ; a collection of
his essays from the Baltimore sun, edited by Andrew   Ciofalo. -- 1st ed.
p.   cm.
"Sunspot books."
ISBN 0-913123-24-2 : $14.95 (est.)
I. Ciofalo, Andrew, 1935-   . II. Title
PN6162.P56  1989
814'.54--dc20              89-11924
CIP

## ACKNOWLEDGEMENTS

All of the essays in this book were previously published in
*The Baltimore Sun*, except for "Of Angels, and Pinheads" and
"Frolicking," which appeared in *The New York Times*.

Special thanks to Claranne Albus, Loretta Bartolomeo,
Judith Dobler Ciofalo, and the Loyola College Word
Processing Center (Nancy Marshall, Marion Wielgosz,
Melia Peisinger and Carla Bundick).

Production of this book would not have been possible without
the support of Dr. David Roswell, Dean of the College of
Arts and Sciences at Loyola College in Maryland.

The overall support of The Maryland State Council on the Arts
and our annual donors underwrites the operations of The Galileo
Press Ltd., a tax-exempt non-profit corporation organized under
the laws of the State of Maryland.

Specific donor support for this book came in the main from
The Greater Baltimore Community Foundation and from the
Noxell Corporation, Dr. Frank C. Marino Foundation and
The Morton and Sophia Macht Foundation.

*The four-year-old found a long feather. It was a blue jay feather. He was excited.*

*"If you have a feather you can fly!" he told me.*

*He held the feather from a hand and ran and flapped his arms. He was a primal creature.*

*I waited.*

*"It's not working," I finally said.*

*He stopped running and looked about.*

*"I need one for the other hand," he said.*

**--Into the Labyrinth**

# FOREWORD

For a decade Carl Pohlner, Jr. has been entertaining and enlightening readers of the Op-Ed page of *The Baltimore Sun* with his witty and insightful essays. Well known to the Baltimore County educational establishment, where he plies his trade as a middle school English teacher and department head, his works are used as models for students being introduced to writing as art.

And Pohlner is a perfect model, writing as he does from common, everyday experiences. He shows us the meaning in the mundane, how to spin an important idea out of the barest threads of experience. That's why professors in the writing program at Loyola College, where students learn that self-knowledge is the precursor of good writing, clip and save Pohlner essays as taut examples of the process. With this book, they now can have a complete set.

Pohlner is a Baltimore institution. His nearly 100 essays in *The Sun* have given him a following that is rare for a local freelance writer. Once, when he spoke his name too loudly in a hospital emergency room, a Towson State University coed came bounding across the room to ask, "Are you Carl Pohlner the writer." Surprised, he could barely muster a "yes" before the feverish young lady excitedly told him about how her high school English class had read his works. Knowing Pohlner, he probably responded the only way that made him comfortable --by offering to buy her a cheese sandwich. He thinks of himself as a teacher and sometime lunch room monitor.

He wonders why all the fuss over a Baltimore County middle school teacher, one whose muse does not stray far from Route I-95 or the Baltimore Beltway. Pohlner's writing station is at a table in the basement of his Harford County tract house, where he sits under a bare bulb, surrounded by cans of motor oil, a bicycle tire pump and other inspirational artifacts from the local hardware store. He'd rather be on some breeze-swept veranda, overlooking a warm turquoise sea and pouring words out of an icy pitcher of some tropical libation. But he's afraid that his dime store muse --you know, the winged plastic Christmas tree topper with the small electric bulb inside-- would never find him there.

Pohlner is most comfortable knowing that he's destined for the pages of a daily newspaper where his work survives the morning garbage through the spectral smudges left on countless fingers. The prospect of such immortality seems to get his creative juices flowing. Those of us who know him worried for his productivity when some years ago he was graduated from newsprint to xerography as professors disseminated his work the only way they could. Having taken well to such permanence, he was deemed ready by The Galileo Press for book-length treatment.

I first became intrigued by Pohlner's work in 1984 when I attended one of the annual lectures he has given to Loyola College freshman composition students. As he explained his creative process, it became clear that he thought and wrote more like a poet than a writer of prose in any genre. An examination of his essays quickly reveals some superficial resemblances: there isn't a logical development that springs from a carefully masked thesis; the beginning of the essay offers no clue as to its ultimate direction or conclusion; there is no conclusion; there are great intuitive leaps between ideas that leave the reader perfectly comfortable; images spin out of images in an almost lyrical fashion. Pohlner has married poetic process and style to prose form and in so doing may have given us a new genre of essay.

Identifiable genre or not, the Pohlner essay owes its form to the Op-Ed page that spawned it. Luckily, Pohlner lives in Baltimore where, in this New Yorker's opinion, the best Op-Ed pages in America are published by the morning and evening versions of *The Sun*, two distinctly different newspapers. A good Op-Ed page is one that isn't dominated by syndicated columns, if any, or even regular columns from the newspaper. It is an editorial agora where knowledgeable citizens exchange artfully expressed ideas for the edification of the entire readership. And it requires a good editor to achieve a balance in the daily contents, cut off an on-going debate before the readers lose interest in the topic, identify ideas and issues that need airing, and nurture those special writers that luck has dropped into the paper's readership area. Pohlner was so nurtured.

Pohlner's poetic herky-jerky style is probably a dictate of the space limitations of the Op-Ed page. No matter what he has to say, he's got to say it in about 750 words. Had Pohlner not found these restrictions comfortable, maybe even inspiring, his writing career might have been limited to lesson plans, or maybe he would have turned to poetry. Obviously, the journalistic environment was his venue.

Journalism exerted two other obvious influences on his work. One is his penchant for research and facts. He spends days doing research before he sits down to write or to explore a new idea that his writing has uncovered. In Pohlner's hands, research is a creative activity; he finds as much wonderment in an archive as in a sunset.

The other influence is that of the audience. It is so general and of such varying educational levels that Pohlner must express the most complex ideas and observations in a way that enables him to speak to as many *Sun* readers as possible. This process of simplification strips the prose of non-essential words and removes the verbal barriers to ideas and feelings that bedevil self-conscious authors.

At the end of this book, Barbara Mallonee, one of the stylish Baltimore essayists herself and a Loyola College writing professor, comments extensively on Pohlner's work. Her commentary indicates why I think that Pohlner's appeal will transcend the Baltimore metro area to wherever ex-urbanites have accepted an uneasy suburban truce under a K mart banner.

**Andrew Ciofalo**
**Editor**

# CONTENTS

## INTRODUCTION

## A RATION OF RED LICORICE

## ADMIRABLE DISORDER

## SEASONS IN MARKED BOXES

## DISTANT BEACONS

## SCHOOL FIGURES

## A LIGHT SENTENCE

## EDITING WATSON

## DEDUCED RECKONING

## ENDPAPERS

# INTRODUCTION

# BEDE'S BIRD

## Introduction to A Feather Short of Flying

In the vestibule of the church just up the street from where I lived as a boy was a button to signal the sorcerer and his apprentice. By what path from the vestibule to the vestry behind the sacrificial altar the electrical current flowed, I do not know. But I imagined it humming in circles around the gold lid of the baptismal font in the vestibule making a warm, glowing sound as when the rim of a goblet is stroked with damp fingers. Then it would ascend in the invisible currents wavering above the red and blue votive lights burning in banks, rising slowly, gathering, and coursing in atomic configurations the halos of statues with ever-still eyes until accelerating aloft and resonating in the military files of organ pipes, from there spewing like cannon fire, forking left and right to the long beams, traveling forward beneath the high windows, at each juncture charging the colored glass --igniting flashes as in a pinball machine-- then rejoining and spilling down into the silver swan's neck of the pulpit microphone, running like spilled holy water enlivened with salt and oil through the crazed rilles in the marble floor of the sanctuary toward the vestry's silence, and there, finally, with sobering obedience to the humble needs of humankind, returning to common bell wires rising behind the wall and, in this ordinary way, making the buzzer rasp hard announcement of the arrival of either an infant, a bride, or a casket, all equally the same to me, inured already at the age of twelve, after four years of service in the manner of an apprentice, to the comings and goings of life on earth.

On this day, wind pushes sun-white clouds in a clear sky. It is cold. The cemetery crew has removed the December wreaths and gone too is a cigar in a glass tube my brother left beneath the wreath. Maybe a clean-up worker smoked it. Good for him. Or maybe it was tossed out with the brown wreaths as the tractor pulling a hopper made its rounds. That doesn't matter. My father would have been proud of my having a book published, the first one to emerge from the family, here in the new country almost a century now. In this place I can wonder to what degree I am an extension of my father, or just what is the source of myself.

I regard now my youth spent in the medieval aura of the church as formative and somewhat druidical, a term denoting almost nothing as the Druids are lost in time, but suggesting mystery and wonder. The church attempted to instruct in the higher end of symbols --water, wine, flame, oil, salt, incense, ashes, the bits of bone and dust buried in the corners of the altar stone-- but the process, I think, worked a bit the other way with me. From lighting fire in midnight winds, pouring cold waters, carrying burning tapers, beholding life and death, preparing cruets of wine and water before dawn in the hollow church reminiscent to me as a boy of Heorot, the mead hall of Beowulf I had read about in a library book, I developed an affinity for the properties of the earth which became more and more alive under rolling waves of incantatory Latin chanted by choirs high in the beams. My paper-thin soul was hammered hard under the raging seas of the "Ora pro nobis" refrain of the Litany of the Saints storming out of the dark ceiling of the church. As a boy, too, I knew from the nuns in the school adjoining the church of Venerable Bede's image of the bird flying out of night into a hall such as Heorot --or the church of my youth in my imagining-- and then flying out again into the dark. And that tenure in the great hall was life. Before daylight I would walk up the street on winter mornings toward the dimly lit church with the wind tearing at my white surplice pinned to a hanger. It would fly behind me like wings or a ghost at my shoulder.

Another formative image I have is of the kitchen of my mother's childhood home, an upstairs apartment in Scranton, where the washing benches from the porch had to be brought in for all of us to sit around the table when we came visiting from Baltimore. The apartment was filled with the kinds of things that make us who we are --a heavy green box with shoe-shining tins and brushes, a closet with two doors that connected the bathroom and the back porch, a coal stove. At one time after the benches had been placed, a large bowl of steaming lima beans was set on the table, the beans mounded high above the rim. On top of the mountain of beans my grandmother placed on a slab of butter cut from the block. As I sat on the rough bench waiting for all to be seated, waiting for all the prayers to be said, ducking the flapping wings of elbows and arms that flew above me, enduring all the confusion it takes for the human species to feed itself, I watched the butter melt. I watched the mass of heroic proportion run endlessly as it turned in an alchemical way from butter to silver and flowed in the pale-green crevices. Benches, food, fire, light --it was all there.

Whenever either my mother or father told a story, it was never more than a recalled image, not even an anecdote --just a memory, a picture hanging on a wall. My father would imitate the sound of his father clearing his throat before he spoke, show me with his fingers how his father packed and tamped his pipe, tell me how his dog shook when the dogcatchers came for it. My mother still conveys bits of dialog, tells of picking berries in the mountains. But that is the stuff of any person; what perhaps made it different was that my parents conveyed to me that it was important. These bits of recollection, told and told again, always evoking an image, contained all the intuitive wisdom --or if that is too strong, all the charm at least-- associated with haiku poetry:

Crowding in the car,
Boys and girls together laugh:
Going to pick berries.

- o -

Father at the landing;
He calls ten names up the stairs--
Children not asleep.

- o -

The truck comes for him.
Standing in the backyard sun,
Old dog knowing, shakes.

- o -

Walking in the dark:
Crossing the bridge from the city
Under a snow sky.

Perhaps even before I knew what a haiku was or even thought of shaping experience in any way, I sensed the larger understanding attached to any fragment of remembered experience, experience that had to be important simply because it was remembered, and made even more important because it was retold. So with a few taps of the keys on a word processor, a few clicks of my fingers to count out syllables (I think I fudged one line), and a smidge of the pidginese we Americans affect when we put on our haiku hats, I have transformed my largely Germanic parents into oriental sages. And I am not certain if the notion is playful or insightful.

As about a hundred pieces of mine appeared over a ten year period on the op-ed page of the Baltimore *Sun*, my parents marvelled at how I had retained so much of the past, and that the most ordinary of events, both past and present, had been given significance. They enjoyed the family-oriented pieces and the memories I had, although they were not very receptive to the satirical or whimsical pieces or to the borderline blasphemies --such as when I depicted the Three Kings sending mailorder cheese assortments on the second Christmas or when I suggested that God may look like a spare part for the Millenium Falcon of Star Wars fame. My mother once told the parish priest that she hated the liberal Jesuits for what they did to my mind at Loyola College. The parish priest said that he didn't think that was a sin because he hated the Jesuits too.

In my wondering fashion I will take a lesson from the sky above this broad field: It is probably wisest for anyone to think they are both like a parent and, even more so, different, just as a cloud reshapes itself in the wind.

Now should I leave a copy of the book here as my brother left a cigar in honor of his son that came --in my mother's old-world perspective-- to take my father's place. I can hear him say, "Don't be a fool! It will just get rained on or someone will steal it!" But if the book were stolen and read by someone, that would be a zen-like glory --just as I hope someone took the cigar and smoked it. I am not sure what to do.

# A RATION OF RED LICORICE

# NIGHT OF WAKING

Night, aegis of half of life, has its reputation for the cruel and mysterious, but is also bears its gifts.

Most of us are day people. Once we are sure it's good and dark, it seems, we turn off the TV, lock the front door, go up the stairs to bed. Then we know, from the sounds of the distant road, that the night-people have moved into their element. But sometimes, day-people are called into the night.

We left the house just before 3 o'clock in the morning. The front street was dark. The stillness was an untouched nerve. Every ordinary sound we made -- the jingling of the car keys, the dull click of the safety locks on the car doors as they were closed-- achieved a deliberateness and intensity in the night.

The headlights, in response to the slight movement of my hand on a dashboard switch inside the dark car, shot suddenly, without any apparent motion, into the yard at the end of the driveway. The red-jewel eye of a rabbit gleamed laser-like back at us.

We slid backwards from the driveway into the street. The twin sluices of light from the car's headlamps ran before us. We followed and were alone. We were a noise the neighborhood would hear in the night.

On the main road, but for a car or two, we were still alone. Along the black road, traffic signals played green-yellow-red to themselves, then played it back again. We came to the glow of lights that was Franklin Square Hospital.

As we drove into this pocket of light and activity in the night, we could hear the chunk-chunk-chunk of an unseen helicopter overhead. In red, green and pulsing blue-white light, it landed almost in our path before the emergency entrance. The sound pushed hard at our ears. There was a swirl of bent, white-cloaked fury at once under the moving blades.

I pulled to the curb at a safe distance from the helicopter and from what was not my business. From the back seat of the car, I took two groggy, pajama-clad children and passed them into the waiting arms of two hastily dressed grandparents. We had called them before we left.

We said goodbye to the kids. Their damp cheeks were stamped with the fleur-de-lys pattern embossed in the vinyl seatcovers. In the emergency room, they took my wife away in a wheelchair.

When I stepped outside to wait until I could rejoin her, the helicopter was still sitting in the landing circle before the entrance. I recognized a teen-aged boy in a white T-shirt who was leaning against the wall. His head rested on the wall. He was staring at the whirling blades of the chopper. For one year, he had attended the school where I teach. Then he left.

His hands were bandaged. Blood was soaking through the wrappings on one hand. He saw me and said, "Hi," without moving his head.

"What happened?" I asked.

"We hit a house," he said. "We were driving down Philadelphia Road and we ran off it and hit this guy's house. The cops made me come here in the ambulance." He told me they were still working on his friend. I wished him well as I remembered having done once before a few years ago. I went back through the glass doors to track down my wife.

When I found her room, I sat in the reclining chair next to her bed. I turned my attention to the suitcase-size monitor on the table next to the bed. This was our third time around here. The monitor was an old friend. He was somewhat a person.

On the long, paper tongue of the monitor, we tracked the frequency, duration and intensity of the contractions. The face of the monitor was a small screen that visually displayed the characteristics of the fetal heartbeat. I reached forward and advanced the audio gain on the monitor to hear its voice. Its voice is the actual sound of the baby's heartbeat. I smiled at my wife and turned the sound back down. She would not smile again for many hours.

In the morning's raw light, I left the hospital. Outside, the helicopter pad was empty. A women in a large hat was standing where the boy with the bloody bandage had been. It seems some unwritten rule of the theater of the night that requires the stage be cleared by dawn.

Just above the trees at the edge of the parking lot, the sun was small, white and hard like the pulp of a green pear. At the car, I did not hear my keys jingle. I did not hear the click of the door's safety lock as I pushed the button down. The night had passed.

(It was a boy.)

# WITH BRIGHT, SHINING FACES

Smell pencil shavings, you smell school. Slam a steel locker door, you hear school. Eat a grilled cheese sandwich that is only toasted on one side --you taste school.

A large yellow bus came down the street. With a wave, my daughter was off for her first day in the first grade.

It all happened too quickly. I had imagined this event as more than a hurried moment culminating in a sulphurous burst of bus exhaust. I had imagined a sad kiss, and a quiet time at the corner for me to play Shakespeare's Polonius: "Lend not thy lunch money to any man, and keep thine own counsel at recess."

But at the bus stop, the neighborhood kids swung their new bookbags into each other's knees as their parents talked about the price of ground beef and took turns telling their children not to sit on the curb.

When the bus rolled its monolithic carriage around the corner, the children cheered. A woman said, "Finally," in the tone of well bent italics.

The kids climbed the steps of the bus and were gone. Before I could find my daughter's face, as I had imagined I would, the bus pulled away. From the rear window of the bus, a child I had never seen before returned my blind salute. I had also done poorly as Polonius. "Take care of yourself," I had said as she crawled into the metal mouth of the bus. Good advice for a six-year-old.

I had stopped in to look around my daughter's school the week before it opened. As I walked about the carpeted first grade section of the open-space school, the only resemblance I could see at first glance between her "area" of the present and my "classroom" of the past was an American flag and a Boston pencil sharpener.

I looked hard for a massive radiator that would clank with steam in the winter and a framed picture of George Washington. It's hard to believe so much could have disappeared in the paltry 28 years that separate our first grade experiences.

Yes, amid the aquarium, terrarium, balance-beam, color TV, overhead projector, headphones and tape gear, there were desks. But their pastel colored tops and stainless steel legs had none of the dark character of my first grade desk.

My first grade desk top was wooden. It was mounted on a black wrought-iron frame of ornate design. The whole business was screwed into the floor.

Each wooden desk top had a hole in the upper right hand corner (left-handers like me be damned) to hold the ink wells. Since ink was only introduced in the third grade then, our holes were empty.

But when I got to the third grade, after two years of fat pencils, the ball point pen had become cheap. The days of the ink well and the splayed steel tip of a real ink pen had blown away. My classmates and I were left again to ponder the vestigial holes in our desk tops, and to wonder what an ink well looked like.

The point of my third grade ball point pen rolled with a chilling rasp on the paper. The ink came out whenever it felt like it. My dominant memory of the grade is of 40 little arms frantically shaking the ink into the tips of their ball point pens between words on a spelling test.

I mentioned ink wells to an old man named John who lives in our neighborhood. He walked with my wife and me down the street after the school bus left.

"When I went to school," he said, "we spit our tobacco juice into the ink wells. That's what they were for."

Then as if to qualify --or perhaps excuse himself-- he said, "Of course, that was in Kansas."

When my daughter returned that afternoon she said, "They gave us these big pencils and the teacher said to have our fathers sharpen them tonight."

I found out quickly enough why the teacher had sent the pencils home to be sharpened. They were too thick to fit into a pencil sharpener.

That night I sat and crudely sharpened her pencils with a steak knife. I watched the lead emerge from the wood and listened to her tell me about her first day in the first grade. In my mind was the image of my own father sitting under the kitchen light with a knife and two fat pencils as I stood by his chair and watched. Ink wells and clanging steam radiators may have walked the path of the dinosaur, but I guess what really counts never changes.

# UPSTAIRS, DOWNSTAIRS

We all need to be alone from time to time. I don't know why. To be alone around my house, I have to stay up after everyone else has gone to bed. One recent night, I tried to do this. I had to outlast the boy's bath, the girl's bath, pleas from kids to stay up late and be alone with me, the baby's last feeding and the surprise reappearance of everyone at once because they all forgot to take a spoonful of green medicine before they went to bed.

Because the medicine had a bad taste, they all stood around in the kitchen sucking on Life Savers and staring at me.

"Why don't you crunch them up real fast?" I said

"We want to suck on them very slowly tonight," Wonder Woman Pajamas said.

"You always say to do that," Superman Pajamas said.

When they left it was quite late and I could tell that I was already too tired to have much fun being alone. But I decided to stick it out. Then, about 15 minutes after everything seemed to have settled down upstairs, I heard a faint and nervous voice from the top of the stairs.

"Daddy?"

"Yes?"

"Are you eating a sandwich?"

"No."

"Well," the voice said with a tremor, "I thought I heard cheese."

"You can't hear cheese," I said.

"Can I come down and check?"

After I successfully defended my solitude against what I recognized at once to be the ancient and intricate Cheese Trick, I returned to the pursuits of the solitary.

I listened to the refrigerator hum for a while. I counted the brown spots on a banana.

I had boxed myself into a corner. I was too tired to read and I couldn't think of a thing to do that would not make noise. I could not play a Bette Midler record, build a bird house --I was not even sure that I could risk making the cheese sandwich which I oddly craved.

Even though everything around my house from the floor boards to the ceiling molding makes noise, I decided to make a cheese sandwich anyway.

I slipped from my stool at the kitchen counter. The stool made a noise. I took one step. The floor made a noise. From upstairs, I heard three bedsprings and one cribspring squeak. I froze. Then, all was quiet.

I opened the refrigerator door. It made a noise and I heard the baby cry out. I turned to stone. In a minute, he fell back asleep. I pushed on and reached inside the refrigerator. A quart of pickles fell on the floor.

By some miracle, the jar lay intact on the floor, but adrenaline was burning in my arms. The jar rocked back and forth. It sounded like a loose cannonball on a rolling deck. I tensed and my ears curled into a fetal position as they waited for the upheaval upstairs.

I was surprised. Not a single bedspring complained. Then I pushed my luck just little too far. I put my hand on the yellow box of cheese and began to slide it from the rack.

"I hear cheese!" a muffled girl's voice cried from upstairs.

"I hear it, too," a boy's voice echoed.

The baby started to cry and I heard the master bedsprings squeak. I knew there was going to be trouble.

"What's going on down there?" the woman's voice said.

"The pickles fell on the floor," I whispered up the stairs.

"Well, the kids said you were making cheese noises. What are they talking about?"

"I don't know," I said. "They are the only people in the world who can hear cheese. Are they taking Zen lessons or something?"

"Are you ready to come to bed yet?"

It was really a strong suggestion hiding behind a question mark. I put the pickle jar away and went upstairs. "I surrender," I said at each bedroom door as I went down the dark hall.

In the darkness, in the silence, I dressed for bed. In the bathroom, I felt for the cup and set the tap at a soft, slow trickle. I tilted the cup so there wouldn't be a splashing noise. I was doing well. A minute later, a voice whispered in the night, "I hear toothpaste."

"I hear it, too," another distant voice said.

# I'VE SEEN IT ALL BEFORE

My sword is not called *Excalibur*. It is called *I've Seen It All Before*. It hangs in the closet with the kitchen broom.

One morning my wife had an idea, the kind of idea that makes my sword hand itch, especially when I haven't finished my first cup of coffee. "Let's go to the zoo," she said.

I ran to the closet with my eyes still closed and began waving *I've Seen It All Before* around the kitchen.

"Well, your other choice for the day," she said as she parried my thrust, "is going to the supermarket for me so I can get some work done around here."

*I've Seen It All Before* fell from my hand and clattered to the floor. The battle was over. I know what going to the supermarket means. It means I will be there forever because I don't know where anything is. Once I went to the supermarket and was there so long I had to stop and buy lunch at the deli counter.

I looked at the baby and he grinned back at me through a mask of oatmeal. His time had come to see a tiger.

"Oh boy! The zoo!" the two older kids said.

We drove to the Baltimore Zoo in Druid Hill Park and we saw the hippos first. I took the baby out of the stroller and held him up so he could see the hippos. He looked at the gold earrings that the woman standing next to us was wearing.

I was not disappointed with his response because he had rewarded me so richly the week before in Ocean City when I gave him his first look at the Atlantic. He had actually looked at the ocean and had actually smiled at it.

Maybe he will like the tigers, I thought. "Let's find the tigers!" I said to the two older children in an effort to generate a little zoo spirit. I knew that the tigers were at the other end of the zoo, but I thought a sense of anticipation might help them enjoy the day. They didn't seem all that excited about the zoo once we were there. "A tiger's skin moves like water when he walks," I said.

"Let's see the tiger's skin move like water!" they said.

The kids liked the flamingos because their legs were on backwards. I took the baby out of the stroller and held him up so he could see the flamingos. He played with my nose.

I am sure that the baby saw the elephants. They are hard to miss. But I think he enjoyed the two fans on the ceiling of the elephant house more. He began to fall asleep after seeing the elephants.

"Let's find the tigers!" I challenged as we stepped into the sunlight and fresh air outside the elephant house.

After we passed the bears and lions, we finally came to the tiger's cage.

It was empty.

"I guess they are inside their den," I said.

"We wanted to see their skin move like water," they said.

"I did, too," I said.

The same thing used to happen to my father when he took me to the zoo --this very zoo, in fact. He always wanted the lions to roar for me, but I don't think they ever did. Usually, when he took me to the lions' cage, the lions were napping in the sun.

The baby had fallen asleep. Maybe he had known the tigers would be out to lunch. He slept all the way home and woke up in his playpen. I am sure that all he knew of the zoo was that he had looked at earrings, a nose, a few fans, and by magic had been transported home in an instant.

That night, when the two oldest went to bed, they wanted to hear about the tigers they had missed. I think they had forgotten they had been to the zoo several times and had seen tigers before.

"Their skin moves like water when they walk," they added. "We don't remember ever seeing that."

"We'll go back some time," I said. "The baby still hasn't seen a tiger."

It seems that even if you have seen it all before, you have to go back and see it three or four times more for every kid you have. After years of looking at whiskers and stripes, that's how I discovered tigers' skin.

# OMENS, RAIN OR SHINE

Old sayings associated with weddings are generally optimistic. They tend to make the best of everything. If the priest is late, the first child will be born quickly. If the groom forgets to shave, the bride's skin will always be smooth. If a dog bites your leg on the way to church, your husband will always be gentle.

You can't lose on your wedding day.

Sunshine and fair weather on a wedding day are usually divined as omens of a bright future. But what happens to the youthful bride who is rattled from her bed by thunder and awakens on her wedding day to a black sky and a torrential downpour?

Does her mother come into her room and confront her with the plain truth? "What a shame. Your marriage is doomed."

Of course not.

When it rains on your nuptials, there is always a grandmother or an old aunt in the wings who will say something like, "Rain means your love will grow." Or, "Rain means you will have many children."

The church roof could fall on your head when you say "I do" and from under a heap of smoking rubble some matriarch would be heard saying, "This means they will have a long life."

My wife and I were married in what the weathermen call "patchy fog."

The diviners of signs and keepers of old sayings in our families perform splendidly at weddings when the weather is plainly fair or foul. But they didn't know what to make of patchy fog. They looked to the sky and shook their heads.

Ever since, our marriage has been closely watched by family soothsayers interested in refining their art by learning the significance of being married in patchy fog.

At the last family wedding, the first to transpire in patchy fog since mine, a murmur ran through the church as the white runner was being pulled down the aisle that this couple was guaranteed at least eight years of marriage and three babies who would cry 24 hours a day until they were two years old. As the organist played a wedding march, another whisper went around the church that they would also have cars that would not run very well.

From time to time during the service, people turned in their seats and stared at me. It is not easy being the father of an omen.

Another bit of optimistic wedding wisdom is that a mismatched couple's marriage will succeed because they will complement each other.

When the parents are pleased with a match, they go about town saying, "They were meant for each other." If the match is horrendous, the parents take solace in the old pre-nuptial saw that differences are healthy because they balance out a marriage. Then the parents go about speaking of all the "doors that will be opened" and of how the young couple will "learn from each other."

I, myself, believe such wisdom to be a cut below whistling in the dark. But it is a popular notion.

Cynics question the optimism that pervades all weddings. They usually slip out to catch a smoke on the church steps half way through the service. I think these spoilsports would like to see the wedding ceremony run, in part, like this:

CLERIC: Can you carry a bike and full diaper pail down the basement stairs at the same time?

BRIDE: I can.

CLERIC: And you, young man, can you replace a hot-water heater while you have the flu?

GROOM: I can.

CLERIC: Can you feed three children a bedtime snack, clean up the mess, bathe them, dress them for bed, tell three stories, help them say their prayers, tuck them in, and then untuck the oldest who forgot to do six pages of arithmetic homework in less than an hour?

BRIDE AND GROOM: We can.

A couple would have to lie like crazy to get through a wedding ceremony like that.

But a wedding is no place for realism. Most people know this. They fill the table, open the liquor cabinet wide, pass out cigars and relish the old sayings that make the best of everything. That's the way it always was and always will be --come rain, shine or patchy fog.

# VAPORIZED, FULL BLAST

I sleep like a log. But it was not until I married and had a houseful of children that I learned it was my greatest failing.

My habit of going to bed at night and sleeping until morning is an unforgivable shortcoming, I am assured by my wife who does not sleep like a log and has to cope single-handedly with all that happens during the night.

Apparently, a good deal goes on. I don't know from personal experience, of course. I am usually told in the morning. Or else I detect a clue, like the door to the medicine chest left ajar.

Some clues are less subtle than an open door to a medicine chest. Sometimes I awaken to find Mickey Mouse bedsheets soaking in the bathtub. Or all three vaporizers running at once. Or my propane torch and a roll of solder on my wife's night-table.

Many years ago, "Good Morning" gave way with me to "What Happened?"

I am told that the only reason I sleep so well is because I place full confidence in my wife's maternal instinct which lets her hear croupy coughs and pillow-muffled wheezes in the midst of sleep.

According to the people with whom I eat lunch, I would hear all the things my wife hears when she is asleep if I had to. I am not so sure about that.

The last time my wife was away spending a few days and nights at the bedside of one of the kids who was in the hospital, I was in charge of hearing the night noises of the other two kids. The idea that a paternal instinct comparable to the maternal instinct would surface in response to a need was dealt a blow.

I awoke on the first morning and thought I had done well until I stumbled into the bathroom to brush my teeth and discovered a puppet on my right hand. I checked the other hand (nothing there), but I avoided the temptation to look at my feet.

When I found the kids downstairs, they said that they had been up for a long time and already had eaten "a few breakfasts." They then described how the wind had knocked over the trash cans and blown the aluminum chairs off the back porch during the night.

I never feel a part of the breakfast conversations around my house because of what I've missed. It makes me feel like Rip Van Winkle. They discuss the sooty bootprints left by the furnace repairman or what the rude woman at the doctor's answering service said.

"That happened?" I will exclaim as I throw down my wall of newspaper.

"Don't you remember?" they say with spoons dripping milk in midair.

"No, I don't," I say.

"You must have been awake! You said 'Snort' when it happened!" they charge with disbelief. "How could you forget--it was awful!"

I would really like to stay awake once to see how it all happens. I get the feeling that at the instant my eyes close, all the lights in the house magically pop on and everyone begins to run about plugging in vaporizers, eating cough drops, phoning doctors and exchanging beds until dawn.

Once, like a kid trying to catch Santa Claus, I lay in bed, fought sleep and tried to stay away all night. I didn't work. In the morning I found myself in the five-year-old's bedroom. The missing kid was down the hall in my bed asleep with a pot under his chin.

"Don't you remember!" my wife said. "It was awful!"

"No, I don't," I said.

"Well, everyone heard you say 'Snort' when you left."

We have had that conversation many times.

# ONE TANGLE AT A TIME

Mine is the job of baiting hooks with bread balls at the pond after supper. I am not very good at it. Even though I seldom look up from my work, I have never been fast enough to have all five hooks in the water at once.

People stroll by where we sit five-in-a-row fishing and say, "If you mix bacon grease and corn meal with the bread, your bread balls will stay on longer."

"Thanks for the tip." I say that a lot when I am fishing.

Real-fisherman types pass and impart real-fisherman-type advice: "Bread balls don't work in this pond. You should use chopped-up weasel noses." They usually show the three little kids a large slippery-looking catfish they have caught, presumably with a weasel nose.

"What would we do if we ever actually caught one?" My wife always asks me.

I am also in charge of untangling things at the pond. Because fishing is such a tangled, advice-ridden thing to do, I am not really all that wild about it.

But it is something a family can do together while the evenings are still pleasant. Fishing might be more fun for me if I went alone and I only had to worry about one bread ball or one tangle at a time. But we always do things together.

Being together as a family is fine, but it isn't always easy when fishing rods are involved.

We did quite a few five-in-a-row things that were not always easy this summer. Going to the ice cream store when it was dark was one of the things we did. Ice cream stores are nicest at night because they always seem to be bright places. We often went to the ice cream store after a tangled twilight fish.

I like ice cream cones because you don't have to put bread balls on them.

But eating ice cream cones five-in-a-row in the chairs along the wall of the ice cream store is a very sticky thing to do. I sometimes think that the only thing more destructive to put in a kid's hand than a fishing rod is an ice cream cone.

That may sound cruel, but at the Newark Howard Johnson's where we once ate five-in-a-row, the youngest covered himself so successfully with spaghetti that people in the lobby sucked in their breath when they saw him as we left.

My wife wipes drips at the ice cream store. She patrols the line with a handful of napkins and does not get to sit down much. I don't feel guilty because I never get to fish much.

The fixtures and walls in the ice cream store are white. At night, the fluorescent lights even make the air look white. People come and go through the door from the dark to the light, from the light to dark. All that is missing is a wooden floor, a screen door and the roar from a large fan on a pole. Despite the mess, you have to take kids to ice cream stores at night so they have something to remember someday, too.

At Ocean City one summer, we sat five-in-a-row on the beach and ate red licorice. We always eat red shoe-string licorice on the beach. Every family has its traditions whose origins are lost. We, also, always take a little plastic potty chair out on the beach with us. The origin of that tradition has not been lost.

We are not really Acapulco-class beach people.

Often when we were sitting on the beach and an airplane flew by towing a sign which touted some Happy Hour or an exotic restaurant, my wife and I would talk about what we would do in Ocean City if we didn't have small children. We would watch the planes fly by as we sat with long red strings hanging from our mouths.

Like a lot of other people, we have to keep reminding ourselves about how good we really have it. Too many people think that if family life is hard or unglamorous, it isn't working. I don't think it is true, but quite a few people do.

One evening when the sand was cool and the beach was empty, we sat five-in-a-row and looked out to sea. We ate a ration of red licorice from our survival kit.

# GREEN BADGE OF COURAGE

I hold the child in my lap.

The young woman holds the syringe with the needle. Another technician swings through the door from the lab and enters the small room. He holds the child's arm. I hold the child's other arm and his chest with one hand.

In his free hand, the child holds a present he can open when this is over. With my other arm I hold his head and force it to the left so he cannot look at his exposed arm.

I have done this blood-drawing business with his older brother and sister. I have done this with him before, but that was two years ago and he does not remember.

I cannot hold the head still enough, and the child sees the needle. I don't like the look of it either. The tangle of arms shifts slightly and tightens again as if the four people were a single creature.

I know they will not find blood the first time, but I can't be sure enough to suggest that they start with the other arm. The last time they searched in both arms until a vein was found. But if I tell them to try the left arm first and they cannot find a vein there, I will feel terrible. It is better to trust their judgment.

The needle enters and the creature with eight arms convulses. The needle searches in the arm. The plunger on the syringe is drawn back and forth. The blood does not slide into the clear barrel of the syringe.

The needle is moved about many times. Fingers push through the tissue on the present.

The progress of the needle is easy to see as it raises the skin. The plunger is drawn back and forth. Dry. Again, dry. Again, dry. Not a drop of blood. The needle comes out.

The arms fall away and the great creature is unformed.

The woman's face gives one flash that is hard to translate. I think her face says, I did not become a lab technician to hurt little children. I am crushed. I am angry. Do not look down on me as I crouch at the foot of your chair as if I am incompetent. All morning long I have drawn blood with ease. It's your child's fault that there was not a vein for me to find.

In a small voice she says, I'm sorry.

Couldn't you tell the right arm held little promise, I think. I told this child the pain would be brief. He was brave throughout the whole thing and now it will have to be done again and his bravery is all used up.

The left arm is wiped with alcohol and the creature reforms. Two more technicians come from the lab and stand ready in the little room. There is no more room.

The needle comes to the arm and the great creature writhes. It talks with many voices. The gift falls to the floor. The needle searches.

The plunger is drawn. Dry.

It searches. Again, dry. It moves again and again. Each time, dry. My eyes never leave the barrel of the syringe. I am looking for blood.

Finally, there is blood. But too little. The plunger is worked. A little more comes. I can tell the woman is fighting for the blood. She is very young. She suddenly withdraws the needle.

That's not enough, I think. What is she doing?

Is that enough, I ask.

Yes.

She fills out a form.

I know what is coming next. She will have to cut a finger tip and draw several pipettes of blood for other tests.

She says nothing and goes on with the paper work.

I wait. Finally I ask, Will he have blood drawn from the finger?

Not after that, she says.

The look on her face does not accord with the act of mercy she offers. But I have given up trying to read the mind of this young woman with long brown hair.

She offers the child a lollipop from a box with hundreds. He takes a green one.

He does not like lollipops and carries it in his hand as he leaves the hospital. The opened gift is in his other hand. I wish he liked lollipops. He should have it stuck to the tip of his tongue like a green badge of courage.

I look down and ask him how he is doing.

It hurted, he says.

He brings it all to a point.

# U-HAUL KIDS

I am thinking about parenting because my wife and I, the two boys and three cats have been exiled to the basement for the evening to allow a teen-age slumber party to come to pass above our heads in privacy. It is my daughter's thirteenth birthday.

My wife is sitting in a lawn chair watching TV; I am typing my thoughts about parenting, and the two boys, 7 and 11, are sitting at the top of the basement stairs waiting for ten o'clock.

They were told that at ten, any uneaten pizza would be slid under the door for them. This was the product of a week of intersibling negotiations, though I eventually convinced my daughter to open the door and hand the box to the boys. At ten, the door opened, a box on the end of an arm shot in, the arm flew back and the door slammed shut. An entire pizza was in the box and the boys were pleased. (My wife had intentionally ordered more pizza than the girls could handle).

My daughter and her friends are wonderful young women. Whenever I see them together, I feel proud. The parents of all my daughter's friends are good people who have worked hard at parenting.

I had seen some of the girls' parents at the soccer field late in the afternoon watching the game. For some of us, it was the third game of the day. At the end of the game one father indicated he was glad the day's driving of kids was about over. When I hesitantly reminded him that his daughter was coming to the slumber party at my house in a few hours, he stoically did not flinch. I felt horribly guilty.

I don't know how the neighborhood mothers can figure it all out. They have conversations that sound like this:

"Will it work if we pull Jason from the choir-practice car pool and put him in the allergy-shot car pool which has to go by the soccer field, anyway?"

"But how would he get to scouts? All the scouts will be with Joan and she isn't leaving until Brendan gets back from trumpet lessons."

"No, they rescheduled the trumpet lesson because of the neighborhood yard sale."

"Then that's OK. But if Bill is driving in the morning for the ballet car pool, there won't be anyone to go into the bathroom with the girls."

"I talked to Susan about that yesterday. When Linda brings Heather and Laura back from baton lessons, she should pass the studio at 11:30, and she's going to stop in and take the girls to the bathroom. We'll just have to explain it to the girls. It will be like the time we had the conflict between gymnastics and First Communion practice and the bishop wouldn't return our phone calls."

"But we still have to work out how we are going to feed them on Saturday."

"Well, Andy ran next weekend's schedule through his office computer, and he said it doesn't look like anyone is going to be able to eat on Saturday."

And this Saturday, something like that did happen. At 2:15 p.m., a father finally found time to feed his small son lunch at the soccer field. It was a foil-wrapped chili dog from a convenience store, the first chance the father and the boy had to stop to eat.

But they hadn't really stopped. The father had driven the boy to the field early to be in a team picture being taken before the game. While the picture was being taken, the father drove to buy the chili dog and brought it back for the boy to eat as he walked from where the pictures were taken to the playing field.

The boy, upset that he would miss the opening minutes of practice, stuffed the chili dog in his mouth and choked on it. A low, brilliant afternoon sun made tears in his eyes continue long after.

I wonder about all this. David Elkind in *The Hurried Child* advises that overstructuring the lives of small children is unhealthy and can lead to problems in early adolescence. And I do know of one family that has structured the lives of their children to the point that I consider it child abuse. That the children are destined to be Olympic medalists does not impress me.

But my daughter and her friends, now entering adolescence, are the product of a moderate amount --by today's wild standard-- of U-Haul parenting. And they are a happy, well-balanced lot. I do not mind hiding in the basement to provide them a party. But with all the driving, complex arrangements and timetables, I am not sure that I am any longer happy and well balanced. There is such a thing as the Hurried Parent, I think. As we structure the lives of our children, so we structure our own lives.

Now we are waiting for 10:30 when we will be allowed up for a powder-room break.

# ADMIRABLE DISORDER

# MR. RABBIT AND THE BEST TRADITION

I am not a man of the soil. I have never put in a crop. Whenever ranchers go to Washington to argue for poisoning coyotes to protect the herds, I sympathize with the coyotes. I also root for wolves whenever they make the news.

Then this spring in a single stroke, my world turned upside-down. I bought a tomato plant. I had to tie it to a stick to make it stand up straight. But I felt a bit lost after that. I left it tied to its stick like Joan to the stake and turned to the books. A most appropriate work presented itself almost at once to my good, soil-stained hand: *The Little Prince*, the work of that mellifluously monikered French air-mail pilot, Antoine de St. Exupery.

This book told of the boy-prince who lived on asteroid B-612 which was about the size of a basketball. He had fallen in love with the single rose that grew on his barren asteroid. He labored greatly to preserve his rose with water and with screens and globes to protect it from the elements. It is a story of a prince who loves a rose, and learns lessons in love and responsibility, amid the foolishness of the cosmos.

This book was some help. Now the matter of responsibility weighed heavily. I had tied the tomato plant to the stake, but what about screens and globes. A weather watch was in order. I went to the kitchen window and checked the sky. I remembered the old saying: Red sky at morning, sailors take warning: red sky at night, sailors delight. The sun was setting but the sky was not red. I looked at the tomato plant tied to the stake under the ominous un-red sky and worried.

The next day over morning coffee with the guys, an old salt (an old history teacher who had been in the Navy) told me that the saying only applied at sea. He said "red sky at morning" was scientifically true, most times, but only at sea. He kept saying *at sea, at sea*. Then he told everyone about when he was in charge of the Shore Patrol in Manila. I sat back. My tomato plant was not at sea; it was in the backyard by the trashcans.

Then a problem appeared. It was a kind of coyote. It was a rabbit.

Mr. Rabbit --as we called him around the house-- was an old friend. We loved him and were proud --in the best tradition of John Steinbeck and Robinson ("I'd sooner kill a man than a hawk") Jeffers-- that he chose to frequent our backyard. But he was nibbling at the tomato plant tied defenselessly to the stake.

In the bubble that comes from my mouth and sits over my head, there was a big black question mark.

At the supper table I said, "Should we go to the expense of barbed wire? Should we set a trap --or poison Mr. Rabbit? No matter what you choose, it's going to cost money. This tomato plant may not be worth the money."

The little children wondered. They said, "We love Mr. Tomato Plant!" Then they said, "We love Mr. Rabbit!"

Out of the mashed-potato-filled mouths of babes came truth. It was an issue which transcended the backyard, but would not transcend far enough to leave us alone. Something was pivoting here like a new, electrically sharpened pencil on a decimal point of consequence.

"What shall it be? The rabbit or the tomato plant? The lady or the tiger?"

"We like Mr. Tiger, too!" they said.

I went back to the books.

This time it was Beatrix Potter's *The Tale of Peter Rabbit*. I would learn the wily ways of the rabbit. I would be a man of the soil yet.

How this all comes out is probably not important. All I can say at this point is that what's left of the tomato plant is still alive. The rabbit watches from the shadows or sits in the sun.

# CHICKEN IN A SWEATER TAKES ALL

The Holy Grail, Prester John and a good crab cake are hard to find. But in my realm of hard-to-find things, worms and rainbows --polar extremes both geographically and aesthetically-- are for me the hardest.

Worms and rainbows are the most elusive only when I am looking for them. This does not mean that my daily rut is strewn with wriggling annelids or that my sky is a panoply of prismatic pizzazz. Rainbows and worms just seem to turn up now and then.

The first time I managed to find a rainbow this summer, a little kid from up the street told me it was supposed to be brighter. He said he had seen better ones in books. I guess rainbows are painted in his imagination in hot limes and cherry reds. I had to admit, as one who hadn't seen a rainbow in a long time, that the colors really could have been a little brighter. Memories are like cheese, I sagely told him. They get better as time passes, but in the end they stink. He got back on his bike and went home and told his mother. She called later to find out what had happened.

Between the pre-Cambrian earthworm and the ephemeral rainbow lie many challenges that range from the simple search for the other shoe to the lifetime quest for a pot large enough to boil a dozen ears of corn or steam two dozen crabs --a pot that will still fit in the cabinet under the kitchen sink. But such things are nothing next to worms and rainbows. I always give doubters 10 minutes to find a worm and 30 days to find a rainbow. I never take their money.

Perhaps the Maryland lottery could be restructured around finding supposedly commonplace things. They could call it Rainbow Roulette and give money to the first so-many ticket holders who come to a claim station with a cup of worms, the maiden name of any one of their four great-grandmothers, or an even number of flip flops. We have seven flip-flops and eight feet in my family. I get to wear the odd one. I call it a flip when I wear it on my left foot, and a flop when I wear it on the right.

On trips in the car we play a game called Finding Things for Points. It's to keep the kids happy. Last week I was dumbfounded that there was not one farm tractor to be seen between Bel Air and Ocean City (we go north above the bay and down through Delaware). As a concession to the three-year-old, I had announced 50 points for a tractor. He would have been better off if I had assigned points for unicycles and pink jeeps. We saw both, and not a single tractor.

We have taken several days trips to Rehoboth and Ocean City this summer, and as a consequence of playing the game we have discovered a real paucity of the predictable between Bel Air and the beach. For instance, there is only one barber pole (Middletown, Del.) to be seen. The Atlantic resorts could capitalize on this: "Come visit us! We're only one barber pole away."

This game, my wife's idea, has an automatic win feature of my own invention. She doesn't think it's good for the children, but I always tell them that the first one who spots a chicken in a sweater wins the game outright and gets a secret prize. My wife thinks the secret prize a cruel trick and that it's potentially damaging to their mental health to have the children always on the look-out for a chicken in a sweater.

But as one who has warred for worms and railed the heavens for the dearth of rainbows, I cannot grasp her logic. I think she may be wrong. I put up 50 points for a tractor on the way to Ocean City and look what happened. And as I lamely cruised the boardwalk that night in my lone flip, I tried to buy a cup of coffee. What a surprise: only one place in a six-block stretch sold coffee (Polock Johnny's). So at least when I'm driving, the old rule stands: A chicken in a sweater takes all. Not everything that is easy to find really is.

Anyone in Baltimore seen an Oriole lately?

# RATATOUILLE WITH WALLACE STEVENS

In these parts, first-frost stalks in sly boots. Preceded usually by a deceptive Indian summer day of Keatsian "mellow fruitfulness" and followed by a day of like poetic merit, first-frost slips in quickly for all of its hollow breadth. It leaves a mold of ice, like niter in a cavern, on paths and walls for us to find in the morning.

This year the warning was a deeper than usual drop in temperature in the dark after supper. That night as I called the kids in for supper, I felt, as I stood at the opened door, the vacuous presence of deep cold. I became suddenly aware of the heat of the just-opened oven behind me.

"It's turned cold," I said.

After supper, we heard the frost warning given on TV. This was a signal to us. It meant the last day for the vegetable garden and a night of making ratatouille, a spicy vegetable stew. We wished we had known earlier of the coming of the first frost so we could have picked-out the garden in daylight. Now it would have to be done by night in the dark.

We dressed the kids warmly in coats they had not worn since last winter. We popped little ski caps on their heads in an assembly line fashion. With flashlights and pans, we went into the yard to strip the plants in the vegetable garden.

It was somewhat an eerie expedition. The beams from the flashlights played ghost-like among the black tangle of falling plants and decaying vines. Most of the wire cages around the tomato plants were askew from wind, rain and neglect. It was good the frost was coming; the garden had lived its season.

Each hard, green tomato and pepper had to be extricated from a Chinese puzzle of string, sticks and chicken wire. We searched at our feet for the last of the zucchini and eggplant. There was more than we expected. Most of what we picked was half grown, but the end had come. The pans filled quickly despite the cold and dark. We smelled wood smoke from the neighbor's chimney.

In the kitchen, the harvest was transferred into three wicker baskets and a large metal tray. The kitchen table was filled. The great mass of shapes and shades of green and the unstudied market-opulence of the scene fell short of comparison. Poet Wallace Stevens wrote in his famous "Study of Two Pears":

*The pears are not viols,*

*Nudes or bottles.*

*They resemble nothing else.*

So it could be said of our harvest of eggplant, zucchini, peppers and tomatoes.

It was this observation that got me thrown out of the kitchen. It was time to cook. The bang of the big pot and a wifely look said, "You and Wallace Stevens go sit in the other room and I'll call you when it's ratatouille time."

Thus I left with an eggplant cradled in hand in the manner Hamlet held alas-poor-Yorick's skull. I would wait.

Ratatouille is a hot vegetable dish combining sliced eggplant, zucchini, green pepper, onion and tomatoes. But it also can be served cold as a relish. Our garden gleanings would be supplemented with store-bought onions and soft red tomatoes pulled from the garden during the last few weeks. We had a big bag of red tomatoes.

I have not always liked ratatouille. Like my first cigarette, my first taste of ratatouille turned me green. Many years ago, a friend forced a cold spoonful of it down me. I called it then (in what might pass now for the waggish vernacular of the Hopkins campus) "rats and tattoos." Since then I have given up cigarettes and taken a liking to cold ratatouille.

Ratatouille would take care of all of the garden leftovers except the green tomatoes. But we had plans for them. On Saturday, we would drive up to the orchard and pick tart, green-skinned apples. The apples and green tomatoes would be chopped, combined half-and-half and, with added spices, be turned into Indian relish.

A call from the kitchen forced me to surrender the eggplant upon which I was metaphysically musing. It was washed, sliced and dropped into the pot. I wondered as I stared into the steaming pot if Wallace Stevens had eaten the two pears after he had written about them.

Eventually that night, it was ratatouille time. The next morning there was frost on the grass.

# A CASE OF RAMPANT CLASS

I don't go out to dinner very often. When I do go, I like to splurge and go to one of those restaurants where they bring the lobsters into the dining room to show you what they look like before they are cooked.

I am a bit provincial. I am easily impressed by a man in a tuxedo waving a wet lobster in my face. It is even more impressive when the man talks about the lobster in a foreign language. Pudge, an eat-drink-and-be-merry acquaintance, recommended a new restaurant to my wife and me.

"Is it the kind of place where they actually show you the lobster?" I asked Pudge on the phone.

"They show you everything," he said. "This place has more class than you can shake a stick at."

"Pudge says this place has more class than you can shake a stick at," I said to my wife.

On the big night, I sat in the bedroom and dreamed of a great Surf and Turf dinner as I pulled on my socks. My wife emptied her purse of its supply of little plastic cowboys and emergency Pampers and we were off. In the warm car, we slid through the cold night.

At the restaurant, we were shuttled away from the dining room that lay behind closed doors to the right of the entrance. There was a sign in the lobby that said, *We Show You Everything*. We were led to the left into the cocktail lounge. The carpet in the lounge was red and the waiters all wore tuxedos.

People who only have a martini or two a year have a right to be fussy. We like our martinis very dry. I know that the only way to get a good martini is to look up at the man in the tuxedo and say, "Give me a water glass full of gin." But we all have to make respectable pretense of liking a little Vermouth.

"Two very dry martinis," I said to the pleasingly sycophantic waiter.

In a wink, a cart rolled up to our table. The waiter poured a touch of Vermouth into two elegant pieces of stemware. Then, with both hands, he took the glasses, held them up, yelled "Pah!" and dashed the contents onto the carpet. With great dignity, he then filled the Vermouth-streaked glasses with gin.

A busboy spied the two wet spots by our table. "Pah and double pah!" he cried and stomped the wet spots on the carpet as he passed with a tray of dishes. It really was a classy place.

After cocktails, we were led back through the lobby with its *We-Show-You-Everything* sign toward the dining room. Visions of Surf and Turf danced in my head. As the heavy oaken doors were being slowly swung open, a cow burst through from the dining room into the lobby. It mooed madly as it roughly circled the lobby.

They really did show you everything here. Into the dining room we marched.

Pudge was a gem. It was fabulous. A waiter, walking in a processional gait with his chin leading his nose, bore shoulder high a live chicken in each white gloved hand. A small pig which had slipped from the grasp of another waiter dashed between his legs, but the waiter with the chickens neither flinched nor broke stride.

Everywhere I looked, wet lobsters were being waved about. I wished I had a stick to shake at all the class. The room was filled with the sounds of mooing, clucking, squealing and live organ music. The man at the organ kept announcing birthdays and playing "Happy Birthday" over and over again.

"I am going to send a note to the organist and tell him it's my birthday even though it isn't," I said to my wife after we had been seated.

"Maybe this place has just a little too much class for us," my wife said as an aquarium full of frogs was wheeled by our table.

"There is no such thing as too much class," I said.

"Then open your menu and look at the prices," she said.

Stepping quickly over a lamb that was loitering in the aisle, we put our shoulders to the heavy doors and fled through the lobby into the night. A heifer seized the opportunity and ran with us.

As we pulled away, a waiter stood in the little light of the restaurant's opened door and waved a wet lobster pleadingly into the darkness.

At home, I broke out some fishsticks and hotdogs; I would have Surf and Turf yet. Still dressed in our finest, we ate in the kitchen.

I guess there really is such a thing as too much class.

# THE LURE OF THE GOLD LINE

Old Scratch was back in town and I was probably not the only one who was tempted to make a devil's deal with the Yankee Mephistopheles at the height of the gold boom in 1980.

At the peak of the flap, I stood in a long line outside the sleazy storefront of a Baltimore gold dealer. I had come to sell two high school rings, my wife's and mine, and a gold coin which I had received when I was christened.

Cartier's in New York advertised that they would help their elite clientele sell unwanted glitter "discreetly." But you had to wait your turn on the street in what had all the appearances of a bread line if you wanted to sell your silver and gold in Baltimore.

After surveying the line, it was my impression that the more you had to sell, the quieter you were.

The man before me in line never spoke a word, never turned around. Because his poker-face seemed at odds with his empty hands, I was sure that he had Krugerrands and commemorative coins stamped with *Your Favorite Vice Presidents* or *Birds of the Fifty States* taped all over his body.

But the woman behind me was friendly and talkative.

"What are you unloading?" she asked.

I showed her my old Calvert Hall ring and my wife's smaller Dulaney ring.

"You should get about 50 bucks for them," she said.

I noted for the first time that like me, my wife had spent a few extra dollars to have her name engraved inside the band of her high school ring. I was struck for a moment at seeing her name carved in gold in its maiden form.

"Is that all you have?" the woman asked.

I showed her my third and most valuable item. It was a 1915 two-and-a-half-dollar gold piece, exactly the size of a dime.

"It looks brand new," she said.

I hadn't noticed that before. I held it up at an angle to the sunlight. She was right. It did look brand new. There wasn't a scratch on it. Its milled edges were sharp.

"My great-grandmother gave it to me when I was christened," I told her. "Outside of a photograph of me sitting in her lap, I have no memory of her at all."

I recalled that the first time I ever saw the coin was when I left home. My mother gave me a little cardboard box then. Inside, sitting on a cotton pad, was the beaded ID bracelet I had worn as a new-born in the hospital, and the gold coin.

As I stood in line, I wondered how it came to pass that a completely unremembered great-grandmother would have an uncirculated 1915 gold piece on hand to give me on my christening in 1945.

I began to wonder if the coin was more than a gift of two and a half dollars. I sensed that the gift may have had something to do with the fact that for 30 years the coin had never been used before it came to me. There was no way of knowing for sure.

"You should get a few hundred bucks for that," the woman said.

"What are you selling?" I asked.

"I have a fork," she said. She pulled it from her coat pocket. "It's silver. My mother and father gave it to me when I was married. It was the only piece I got. What good is one fork?"

"Do you have anything else?" I asked. She saw me look at the bulge in her other pocket.

"It's a can of wasp spray," she said as she slid the can out an inch. "I thought there might be trouble with all this gold and silver around."

I showed her the little red tack hammer I had in my pocket. I had taken it from a counter drawer in the kitchen before I left.

"Do you have any regrets about selling your fork -- since your parents gave it to you?" I asked.

"When the family heirloom is a fork, I think I'll take the money," she said.

My mind leaped into the future and I saw her children in a lawyer's office as her will was being read. I could see a strong-box being opened and the fork being presented to the oldest surviving child.

Maybe some things should be sold. But I had some doubts about my three lumps of gold.

I said goodbye to the woman with the fork and left. At the corner, I stopped and looked back at the gold line. The woman was standing behind the silent man who had the *Birds of the Fifty States* taped to his body. My place was gone.

When I got home, I put the two high school rings back in the small chest where we keep such treasures. I returned the gold coin to the little white box with the cotton stuffing. I carefully placed it inside the ring formed by the bracelet of beads which said "Boy Pohlner."

I put the tack hammer back in the kitchen drawer. The gold rush was over.

As I closed the drawer with an air of finality, my daughter came bouncing into the kitchen.

"Have you seen my gold Brownie pin? she asked.

"I'll look around," I said.

After she left, I began to fish in my pocket. I had forgotten about that.

# FRANKENSPEED ON URETHANE

"Mr. Speed! Mr. Speed, clear the floor! This is not an *All Skate*. This is for couples only!" the young man at the microphone called over the loudspeaker.

They turned down the lights at the roller rink. Mr. Speed, dressed in a three-piece suit, slipped off to the side and tapped at his damp brow with a handkerchief. Fifty grade-school kids paired up and wheeled about in the spinning motes of colored light that swirled on the floor from the great spinning ball overhead.

It was 4 o'clock on a Wednesday afternoon, the one weekday when the roller rink opened in the afternoon and when they offered a special discount price. Every Wednesday the place filled with little kids from the nearby schools. Their mothers, with laps full of jackets and shoes, sat on the side and talked. And then there was Mr. Speed in his suit who sailed among the little kids like a giant.

Before this afternoon, Mr. Speed had not been roller skating since a cold Friday night about 20 years ago when he last went to the old Carlin's roller rink with his church youth group. That was when a winter's night ride on a rented bus from Baynesville into Baltimore was a great adventure. His group rented a bus once a year and went to Carlin's. It was something to look forward to.

Back then, Mr. Speed thought himself a gay-wheel of a fellow, though he did look with awe at the Fonzie and Laverne-and-Shirley types who, dressed in bright silk jackets and short skirts, skated backwards and acted like they owned the place.

But he knew one thing: He could skate without falling down and he could cross his legs in the turns, which was more than many of his friends could do. The Silk Jackets and Short Skirts had to respect him for that, he used to think as he took to the floor in a flannel shirt and pushed his eyeglasses back up to the bridge of his nose. At Carlin's, he bounced and swayed to the live organ music as his wooden wheels thundered over the hard boards.

"All skate! It's an *All Skate* now," the loudspeaker said as the lights came up and the swirling motes from the silver ball faded.

Mr. Speed pushed himself back onto the rink and his orange urethane wheels swished on the gray urethane-coated floor. Overhead, starbursts of colored lights flashed and a pair of squad car lights rolled red-white-and-blue. The music was disco. Mr. Speed bent and crisscrossed his legs in the first turn and flew with only a wobble or two down the far side of the rink.

Bright-colored silk flapped in his mind as he rocketed forward. From behind, a pack of first-graders came up even with him at the second turn and shot by *en masse* like so many Lucys and Linuses. One voice said, "Hi, Daddy."

Mr. Speed could feel that it would not be long before his legs fully remembered what his mind recalled so well. As he came down the near side of the rink, his wife called to him, "Why don't you take off your coat and..."

But that was all he heard. He was already into the turn and crossing his legs back and forth like hungry scissor blades. Mr. Speed was not sure if he liked the slightly sticky sound and sensation of urethane on urethane. But the combination did not seem to him to slip the way wood on wood often did. In a little drawer in his mind was permanently filed the scraping sound of wooden skate wheels starting to give way in a turn on the hardwood floor at Carlin's.

"Trios! Trios!" the loudspeaker announced as the light behind *All Skate* on the signboard went dark and *Trios* flashed on. Phooey, thought Mr. Speed, who was just getting up steam. The lights dimmed and the silver ball rained a storm of color onto the floor. The little children, including his daughter, linked hands and circled in threes like pieces of a broken necklace of beads.

Mr. Speed coasted off the rink and stopped with a little swirl as he stepped onto the carpet. "Drat," he said to his wife who had a baby over her shoulder and a four-year-old on skates clinging to her leg for support. "Whenever I get going, they always change the sign to *Couples* or *Trios*," he said. He gave a push and moved away over the carpet.

"Where are you going?" she asked.

"I want to look at the skating jackets in the showcase," he said.

She had already begun to regret that she had given him that look the night before which said: Why don't you leave work a little early tomorrow and meet us at the roller rink so you can see how well your children can skate. There was something coming over him, she sensed.

Mr. Speed returned and stopped with a little swirl. "There's a pink one over there with a purple lightning bolt that only costs 60 bucks," he said as he bounced to the disco beat.

Yes, she thought, it may have taken Mary Shelley but an evening and a few strokes of the pen to create Frankenstein, but with just one rued look, she had created Mr. Speed.

"Look! It's an *All Skate*," Mr. Speed said as the baby began to cry. His eyes blinked pink as he dashed off. He felt purple thunderbolts fly from him and he heard them spark as they fell on the scorched floor behind him. In the electric hum of urethane on urethane, he was gone.

# FROLICKING

I went to a pool party even though I find swimming pools boring.

Swimming pools bore me because I am very poor at frolicking. I think you have to frolic well to enjoy them.

I like to swim in the ocean where the surf knocks you about and a stiff undertow provides a little adventure. After I jump into a swimming pool, I can never think of much to do.

At the party, I guess I was standing glumly in the pool like a six-foot stick in a tub of chlorinated mud as my host passed above me with a tray of drinks. "Frolic! Frolic!" he said in the same way that my mother still says, "Eat! Eat!"

I did a bit of a sidestroke across the pool and back again to show my appreciation for his hospitality.

I once had a neighbor who was good at frolicking. Whenever he shoveled snow, snowball battles involving most of the block would break out. When he raked leaves, a few dozen kids and most of their parents would be in his yard jumping in the piles of leaves. He could not wash his car without starting a hose fight with other neighbors. I used to be afraid to go out and get the mail when I saw him around.

A lithe, bronze-colored young woman with a beach ball jumped into the pool next to me. She smelled like a coconut. She pushed off a few feet and held up the ball. "Catch!" she called to me. She threw the ball and I caught it and threw it back to her. Then she turned and threw it to some guy she knew and swam off.

I guessed that counted as a frolic and I hoped my host had been watching.

I think that people are put under a lot of pressure by advertising to frolic. Frolicking is held up to us as the norm.

A bikini-clad girl riding a horse in the surf sells cigarettes. Guys who have just sailed around the world in a small boat come to land and, like the Pilgrims I suppose, celebrate by throwing beer cans at each other.

There is even a series of television commercials that encourages you to switch to decaffeinated coffee if you are too tense to frolic. Heaven help you if Robert Young catches you not smiling when the septic tank backs up.

"Darn and double darn," says the unfrolicsome fellow in the TV commercial as he gets out of his car and his transmission drops into the driveway.

"What's wrong, Fred?" says Robert Young with a concerned look, as he puts his arm around Fred. (This is where I would sock him in the nose.)

"It's his nerves," Fred's wife butts in. (It's really his transmission.)

"You should switch to decaffeinated coffee," says Robert Young.

The scene then changes to some time in the future when Fred is better able to cope with life because he switched to decaffeinated coffee.

Fred's dog jumps onto the dining room table and steals a roast beef, but Fred, his wife and Robert Young just chuckle because they are drinking decaffeinated coffee. They think the dog is cute. They fill their cups again in anticipation, I imagine, of another tragedy.

I am not knocking frolicking. It's just that I am bad at it and I didn't want my host to think I wasn't enjoying his party.

His party was starting to look like that glossy vodka advertisement that features people in modish swim togs reveling around a swimming pool while they drink everything from Kool-Aid to bath water with a splash of vodka in it. I climbed out of the pool and went over to a tub that was full of ice and canned beer. "Let me get one for you," a young fellow said who was standing by the tub with his buddies.

He shook the can, then popped the top so that a geyser of foam flew all over me and everyone else.

"Thanks," I said as I reached for the can.

"We only go around once," he said.

"I hope we make it," I said.

Back by the pool there was a lot of noise. The bronze beauty who smelled like a coconut had ridden a horse onto the diving board and was waving to a guy who had just landed a hang-glider on the garage roof.

"It's just like TV," my host burbled as he rushed by.

Maybe I should switch to decaffeinated coffee.

# LOW ROLLING

Our bus driver to the land of whirling oranges and plums seemed to be a sharp fellow. He told us that the slot machines at entrances and at ends of aisles are set to pay off more frequently than the other machines. This is to lure passers-by into the deep files of cranks and slots.

That seemed to be the case at the three casinos in Atlantic City my wife and I visited the other afternoon. Like many who live here in the East, we had never been to a casino before.

As you walk the aisles in the casinos, all you see and hear is money dropping and clattering from the machines that flank you. But a cherry or two coming up frequently, followed by a handful of coins dropping into a trough, doesn't mean --as we found out-- that you have a better chance of coming out ahead. All it means is that the aisle machines take a little longer than the others to eat all your money.

But for a low roller like me, who came to the glitter-pits of the East with lunch sandwiches secreted in the side pockets of his suit jacket, the frequent pay off of the aisle machines provides a little excitement.

Nevertheless, losing my money in the casinos was not as much fun as everyone told me it was going to be.

I am the kind of person who slips from a stool at a $2 blackjack table and says, I could have had an oil change and a lube for what I just lost. But people who really enjoy gambling don't seem to think of things like that.

I believe that gamblers have souls far more pure than mine could ever hope to be.

They do not worry about such base things as oil changes. They are satisfied with the beauty of a moment's thrill at the turn of a card. I did my best the other day in Atlantic City, but I guess I just don't know how to get a kick out of throwing money around.

I think my parents tried to teach me how to throw money around when I was a kid, but it didn't work. A few years after V-E Day, they bought me a book called "Bobbie Had a Nickel." They were proud that I quickly memorized the versified story about a boy and his nickel and that I could recite it before what must have been terrifically enthralled family audiences at grandmother's house on Sunday nights.

The book (which is still in print) is about a red-haired boy named Bobbie who tries to decide how to spend a nickel which has an Indian on the front and a buffalo on the back. After sifting through many illustrated choices, which include such real items as a bean bag and a pin-wheel, Bobbie finally chooses to spend his nickel on a bit of ephemera --a ride on a carousel. The book ends with a question: Would YOU have done the same?

Of course not, was what I thought as a kid: A carousel ride lasts two minutes, but a bean bag is a joy forever.

My parents encouraged me to see the beauty in Bobbie's choice. They explained how an evanescent pleasure such as a carousel ride can be as rewarding as the delight which comes from owning something real, something material --like a bean bag. The lesson was lost on my young but hard-bitten Yankee soul.

I thought about Bobbie's carousel as I stared at a spinning roulette wheel the other afternoon. I thought of Bobbie's nickel as I clutched a five-dollar bill that would buy the one minimum-bet chip I needed to "ride" the wheel. The old words came back to me:

> *Bobbie sat and wondered,*
>
> *Bobbie sat and thought-*
>
> *What would be the NICEST thing*
>
> *A nickel ever bought?*

"Maybe I shouldn't do this," I said to my wife. "With this five-dollar bill, I could buy us each a chair to sit down in for 15 minutes."

You see, there are no chairs or benches in the casinos.

If you wanted to sit down at the casino where I was contemplating playing roulette, for instance, you had to go into a lounge off the casino floor to find a chair. All drinks cost $2.50 in the lounge and they barely wet the glasses. There is a card on each table which says you must buy one drink per person to sit in the chairs. When the lounge has some sort of musical attraction, according to the card, you are required to buy two drinks per person to sit in the chairs.

At the time, I didn't hear anyone singing in the lounge so I knew that if we hurried we could sit down in a chair for only five bucks. I looked hard at the spinning roulette wheel.

Given the choice of a moment's splendor or a chair, I chose the chair. It was the most I got for my money all day.

# WIRE WORK

Although I like campfire beans and sleeping under the stars, I'm glad I'm not a cowboy. I wouldn't like to have to string or mend wire fences.

Or was it the sheepmen who made the fences and the angry cowboys who tore them down?

It doesn't make any difference. I wouldn't like to tear down wire fences either. I don't like to work with rolls of wire fence because they refuse to unroll, they cut my hands and, once opened, recoil around me and trap me inside.

It's not that I don't like fences. Everyone likes fences. It's anything that comes in an uncooperative coil that I don't like. Battery jump cables, clothes line, Christmas tree lights and garden hoses are a few of my other enemies.

The other day, I was forced to wrestle with a large roll of wire fence. It was supposed to be a nice spring day, but as soon as I appeared in the yard with my roll of fence, wire cutters and nails, the temperature suddenly dropped and a gusty, annoying wind began to blow. The one advantage primitive man had over modern man, I think, was that he knew an omen when he saw one.

Despite the difficulty I had in working with my roll of fence, I was able to console myself with the thought that making a fence was an ancient and time-honored thing to do and probably was a part of being a man.

Men have always built fences. Stone fences were made where stones were found and wooden fences were made where there was ample timber. Where there was only sod to be found on an empty prairie, fences were made with mounds of sod. Mother Nature would have to get up mighty early to frustrate man's inimical urge to make fences.

Oddly enough, many people think it was Robert Frost who said, "Good fences make good neighbors." As I labored in the yard with my roll of fence, I could not help thinking of Frost's "Mending Wall" which contains the famous line. Actually, it is Frost's neighbor in the poem who says that good fences make good neighbors.

Frost whimsically chided the neighbor for his unthinking faith in an old saying as they walked on either side of a stone fence in spring repairing the ravages of careless hunters and winter weather by replacing fallen stones. The neighbor is presented as creature of the stone age as he lifts the rocks that have fallen on his side of the fence. "He moves in darkness as it seems to me," says Frost.

But fences aren't always dark things. My favorite fence was the great stone fence my wife's grandfather built behind his 200-year-old house on Roast Meat Hill in the Connecticut woods. On Roast Meat Hill, fences were made with stones because you didn't have to look far to find a rock.

His fence was made with piled rocks and it was about three feet high and two feet thick. It served no other purpose than to separate the part of his property he planned to mow from the acres of wilderness he didn't plan to do much about. It was a good fence because when he wanted to barbecue a steak, all he had to do was remove a few stones from the top it, build a fire in the hole and cook the best fence food ever. Robert Frost wouldn't grumble about that fence.

The fence I was building the other day in the cold and wind was merely an enclosure around the deck in the backyard. I turned the deck into a wire pen so our youngest will not fall off this summer. We hope he can be put outside to play by himself. Knowing him, I hammered in two nails wherever one was needed, until I had a fence that was, in the century-old phrase of the first promoters of barbed wire, "Horse high, pig tight and hog strong."

One of the older kids looked at all the wire work when I was finished and said that maybe now we could "get our own personal cow." I shook the fence and it occurred to me that it was not a bad idea.

You get to thinking like that after a day of hammering wire against wood and thinking about being a cowboy.

# TO BED, TO BED

When the moon is a distant mothball of ice and the dark is brittle with cold, there is no better place to be than in bed.

I am glad that I am no longer young and foolish and obligated to run around town till all hours. On long winter nights, I like to turn down the heat till the floorboards are chilly and go to bed under a club sandwich of blankets, quilts and afghans knitted by grannies.

Quite understandably, one of my favorite paintings is Norman Rockwell's "Crackers in Bed." It depicts a youth eating crackers and reading by lamplight in a bed heaped with blankets. Winter stars can be seen from the window in the boy's room

Rockwell did the painting in 1921 for an advertisement for the Edison Mazda Lamp Works. But what the painting sells me today is the old-fashioned comfort, if not virtue, of staying home and going to bed.

Louis XIV, a man of my own temper apparently, had 413 beds. I don't have that many beds, of course. I have one bed, but it's a good bed. As a child, I was taught the value of buying a good bed by the neighbors across an alley who suffered from the inadequacies of their mattress.

On quiet summer nights, I would peek from my bedroom window and partake of the grand commotions raised by the frequent midnight rotations and flippings of their miserable mattress. They would argue. They would knock over tables and lamps. Their dog would bark. They fought the battle of shifting hills and valleys. In the night, I could hear them beating down lumps with their fists.

Though being snug in bed is a pleasant way to pass a winter night, getting to bed can be difficult.

When you are dog-tired and content in your chair, who wants to get up and go to bed? It is usually at the end of the 11-o'clock TV news that I, sunk deeply in an overstuffed chair and warmly covered with newspaper, encounter the final and most difficult task of the day. Going to bed.

*Must we go to bed indeed? Well then,*

*Let us arise and go like men,*

*And face with undaunted tread*

*The long black passage up to bed.*

That is a bold challenge from Robert Louis Stevenson.

Often as I have sat, trying to muster courage to go to bed, wild thoughts have come to me. I have imagined a Tom-Swift hydraulic system that would raise my chair through a trapdoor in the living room ceiling into the bedroom overhead. At its peak the chair would tilt and drop me into bed.

I have even thought of a bedtime invention called Spray-On Pajamas for people like me who are often too tired to face what it takes to dress for bed. Spray-On Pajamas would be a sticky fuzz you would spray on yourself until you looked like a teddy bear. It would come in an assortment of designer colors and designer insulation ratings. The stuff would rinse off in the morning shower.

Some people avoid the rigors of "the long black passage up to bed" and don't go to bed; when they get tired, they just fall asleep wherever they happen to be in the house. No matter how strong my urge to stay put and let soothing colored photons from the TV wash over me through the night, I am just not bohemian enough to sleep in my chair.

The free spirits who just drop in their tracks when overwhelmed with sleep are lucky in that they can avoid the many rituals that are a part of a formal going to bed. They don't have to take out the trash or check locks. They don't have to assault their nepenthean tranquility with an eye-watering atomic-mint toothpaste. They don't have to curse and start over when they look in the mirror and see that their pajamas are on inside-out.

But what they do miss are the comforts of bed. It is not until you finally dance across a cold floor in bare feet, jump into bed and cry, "Made it!" that the price of going to bed ever seems worth it.

# COSMIC LEVITY

Accordion popcorn is what I make on Friday nights.

You make accordion popcorn by putting too much --way too much-- popping corn into the pot. It's that simple.

As the kernels explode faster and faster and the pot fills, the lid lifts an inch, then another, then another, and then many more.

The popping sound grows firecracker loud once the lid begins to lift and you have to keep your wits about you. I hold tight to the pot handle and ever-rising lid until the popping stops.

Then you have, in careful balance, an accordion of popcorn.

It is my favorite way to make popcorn, but my wife doesn't like it when I go too far in flourishing the pot and saying, "Voila!" and the accordion collapses. My small children observe the weekly making of accordion popcorn with a mixture of delight and fear.

Sam Bear is my popcorn hero. He is a little bear and main character in Frank Asch's illustrated book *Popcorn* which I read often to my 3-year-old. When Sam's parents go out one night, he throws a party for his friends and he tells everyone on the telephone to bring something good to eat. All of his friends arrive with bags and boxes of popping corn which they pop all at once in an enormous kettle on the kitchen stove. As the pages turn, the house fills with popcorn till it blows out the chimney and onto the lawn.

But the charm of the story seems lost on the 3-year-old. Being raised in a house where accordion popcorn is made once a week, he finds the story plausible enough and does not laugh the way the author intended. Sensing my fondness for the story, I think he fears that I will find an even more magnificent way to make popcorn than accordion popcorn.

Such a concern would be legitimate because I have always wanted to obtain dried ears of popping corn so I could try making popcorn the way some early American Indians did --by holding a full ear over a fire with tongs. If I could get popcorn on the cob, Friday nights in the kitchen would never be the same.

Unfortunately, you can't pop the dried kernels of the ordinary cob corn we eat during the summer because it isn't hard enough. Popcorn is a harder, starchier variety than sweet corn. When popcorn is heated, its internal moisture turns to steam that is not slowly leaked because of the hardness of the kernel. The pressure builds until the kernel explodes and turns itself inside out.

Popcorn is old stuff. It is not the product of crossbreeding, a manmade food novelty. It occurs naturally and therefore must play some part in the order of the universe. Popcorn over 5,000 years old has been found by archaeologists.

On one of his voyages Columbus encountered Indians, as he thought them to be, wearing popcorn in an ornamental fashion. According to Tomie de Paola's *The Popcorn Book*, Columbus also observed the Indians of the New World vending popcorn, which creates in my mind a picture of vendors scurrying about crying, "Popcorn! Get your popcorn!" as the natives gathered on the beach and watched the longboat being lowered from the *Santa Maria*.

The Iroquois, says de Paola, made popcorn by stirring kernels in pots of hot sand; they also concocted popcorn soup and brought popcorn as a gift to the first Thanksgiving. He says that the colonists eventually took to eating popcorn mixed with cream for breakfast. That may sound repulsive, but imagine what a pilgrim would think of a bowl of Trix.

*The Popcorn Book* is a brief children's book but it is, as far as I can tell, the only book catalogued by Maryland libraries that is devoted completely to popcorn. Popcorn seems to be kid stuff. Weathering the suspicious glances of mothers with children in tow, I read the book in the children's section of the Bel Air library at a very small table.

Later, in the adult section of the library, I found that the *Encyclopaedia Britannica* contains no entry for popcorn and no entry for corn. It contains no entry for popcorn, of course, because the British are stuffy people. But it contains no entry for corn because outside the United States corn is used as the generic name for all cereal grains. You can read about what we call corn under the heading Maize. Under that heading, the *Britannica* refers to popcorn as popcorn and not, as I expected, popmaize.

Corn is a New World food and a dietary staple in the Americas. But what part popcorn, the exploding variety, plays in the order of things may never be determined. I think the cosmos provided us with popcorn, more than likely, just for fun. Perhaps it is a token of cosmic levity. A universe with popcorn can't ultimately be cruel at heart.

Though my wife and her kitchen broom think differently.

# STUMPED

Armed with a bladed iron bar, I felt like a primitive as I stood with a dry mouth and surveyed the woods.

I had weakened quickly and I kept my eyes peeled for an attack. If fur-clad men reeking of grease and smoke came from anywhere, I thought, it would probably be from the gorge beyond the woods where the water runs. I imagined them tripping over wagons and bicycles as they came through the woods toward the house.

I returned to my work and threw the man-high shaft down at a tree root with a grunt. I was removing another stump.

I was tired and my arms shook as I worked to unwedge the blade from a cracked root. With the strength I had left, I would have to wait until a feral marauder came close enough that I could drop the massive iron bar on his foot.

You get primitive thoughts when you chop at tree roots with an iron bar, especially when the woods are quiet like the beginning of time and haunted with sunset colors.

My wife and I had always wanted a wooded yard, but we may have bitten off more wood than we can chew. Ever since we moved here a decade ago, I have been felling trees and pulling stumps.

In spite of the deference traditionally accorded the stone wall for its unyielding nature, I think that tree stumps are harder things to budge.

Confederate General Stonewall Jackson might have been better complimented had he been called Treestump Jackson.

President Andrew Jackson was close to the ultimate in monikers for the staunch and intractable with his arboreal appellation Old Hickory. But we have yet to have a leader sufficiently stolid and tenacious whom we could fondly call Old Stump.

President Nixon came close during the Watergate investigation, but when the chips were down, he faltered and stonewalled when he should have stumped.

George Washington had his big chance when he chopped down the cherry tree, but he apparently walked away from the stump. His father probably spent weeks uprooting it with an iron bar.

Years ago when I began battling tree stumps in my yard, I found myself giving up pretty easily. I was guided by a war-college maxim: When confronted with a problem that can't be solved, change the problem.

Whenever I met a stump that wouldn't let go of the earth, I would change the problem by trying to find some good use for the stump. Once an old stump the size of a trashcan fell into disfavor with the family and I was petitioned mightily:

"It's right where first base is supposed to be!" the boy said.

"It's right where I want to jump rope!" the girl said.

"It's exactly where the picnic table should be!" my wife said. She said this many times.

Never had a treestump contributed so greatly to the unhappiness of mankind.

"Let's do this," I said as I thought deeply. "Let's nail some wire to the stump and plant ivy. When the ivy grows up a bit, I can prune it so it looks like a duck or something."

There was a prodigiously negative outcry and my plan for an ivy duck was scuttled.

I rented a chain saw and cut the stump, but that didn't work. What needed cutting was under the stump.

I drilled holes in the stump and bought expensive chemicals to pour into the holes. The chemicals were guaranteed to work. On the package was a picture of a stump withering away. The chemicals did not work.

I poured kerosene into the holes and set fire to the stump. For months, fires burned and burned till I had used all the kerosene. But whenever the smoke cleared, the stump was always there.

For two years, chain saws were rented, holes were drilled, chemicals bought and fires set. Nothing worked.

In the third year of the greatest stump war I had ever waged, I went to work on the black and shattered monolith with a simple iron bar. During the summer of that year, I got to know every tough wooden detail of that stump. I eventually succeeded in uprooting it.

But during the long years of that stump war, the boy had found another place to play ball. The girl had found it better to jump rope in the driveway. A third child, who had been born and attained the age of three during the campaign, had learned to live around the stump. And all of us had grown used to having the picnic table somewhere else in the year.

I had won some sort of primitive victory. But what remained was a very purposeless black hole and empty place.

I have come to think, lately, that it was just the spot for a stump.

# SPICE OF LIFE

Henry VIII once received a pair of clock socks as a precious gift from Spain.

They were long stockings richly embroidered with clocks. In the days of Henry there were no preppies and little alligators, but it was quite the rage among dandies and fine ladies to have clocks on their socks.

I don't know why. But I am glad it is not the fashion today.

I prefer plain socks and, actually, I have never worn socks of any other color than black.

This may be considered at first to be a sign of a melancholic disposition, but that is not the case at all.

I have always worn black socks for practical reasons.

It is effort enough to get a shirt and tie reasonably coordinated in a dark bedroom in the morning without having to guess which socks in the drawer are black, brown, forest green or navy blue. In dim light they all look the same.

If all your socks are black, a basic color that goes with anything, all you have to do is reach in the drawer, grab two socks --any two socks-- and you are on your way.

Also, if all your socks are black, you don't have to worry about matching them and folding them in pairs when the socks are brought upstairs from the laundry for everyone to claim and sort. My wife and kids spend hours matching and folding socks:

"Does anyone see a brown sock with a red strip but without any white stripes!"

"Does anyone see a white sock with ladybugs!"

It goes on and on.

I am always the first one done. I just easily fish the black ones out of the basket, toss them into the drawer in a gorgon-like lump and walk away.

"That's unfair!" the kids always cry as they rummage through the basket up to their elbows in colorful socks.

My time-saving system of wearing only black socks works best if all the socks are of the same age. Otherwise you run the risk of wearing a thin balding sock with a fluffy new sock, which can give you a lopsided feeling.

That is why I replace my collection of black socks in its entirety every two years.

Through the years I have found that men who buy 14 pairs of black socks at a clip are often mistaken for clergymen.

"Here you are, Reverend," the saleswoman usually says as I am handed my bag of socks.

"Bless you, my child," I always say.

It is unkind to tamper with an innocent person's perception of reality.

But as I was setting forth on my most recent trip to buy a two-year supply of black socks, I gave some thought to changing colors.

"Why don't you get a different color and spice up your life?" the kids suggested. They are always after me to "spice up" my life.

"Get green socks so you will always feel like you are walking through grass," one said.

"Get blue socks so you will feel like you are wading in the ocean," another said.

These seemed to be good ideas.

But I lost my resolve when I got to the store and I began loading my arms out of habit with black socks. Then, as I stood at the wall rack trying to find a fourteenth pair of black socks, my eye was caught by a column of fiery red socks.

"Maybe a pair of those would spice up my life," I thought.

The one thing more unusual than a man approaching a cash register with 14 pairs of blacks socks is a man with 13 pairs of black socks and one pair of red socks.

I nervously held the red socks in my hand under the counter as the young salesgirl counted the black socks. I still wasn't sure I should buy them.

Then, when the socks were almost counted, I pulled the red socks from under the counter like an ace from the hole and plopped them on top of the pile.

"Why, Reverend!" the girl gasped.

She blushed, I blushed. I will never buy a pair of red socks again.

The red socks now sit in the drawer, a scarlet presence, pulsing whenever I open the drawer like the heart of temptation. I haven't had the courage to wear them.

As for spicing up my life, I will await the return of socks with clocks.

# THE STING

Yellow jackets seem to annoy us most in autumn.

At the Double-Tee Burger in Luray, Virginia, we went to get into the car with trays of burgers and fries, but yellow jackets were in the car. I set the cardboard trays of food on the roof of the car and tried to chase out the yellow jackets by taking a window-wiping rag from under the front seat and waving it about.

As I was doing this, other yellow jackets began working at the food on the roof of the car. Yellow jackets also flew around the heads of the kids like angry electrons.

When I finally got all five of us safely inside the car with windows tightly rolled up and an Indian-summer sun making us perspire freely, I realized that the trays of food were still on the roof of the car.

A smart person would have pulled out of the parking lot and left a trail of splattered milkshakes and wind-blown french fries on the streets of Luray. But I went forth with the window-wiping rag and fought another long and complicated battle with the yellow jackets.

It was not long before this that we were in Waynesboro, Virginia, and engaged in a war with yellow jackets at the Waynesboro Motor Lodge. It was my fault that yellow jackets attacked us there. I didn't know that yellow jackets fancied anti-freeze.

Just before the family began hauling suitcases out of our room to the car, I decided to check the radiator. A few drops of fluid fell from the radiator cap and yellow jackets were there at once.

The old woman who was pushing a linen cart from room to room marveled at the number of yellow jackets and handed me a spray can from her cart.

"Maybe this'll fix 'em," she said.

I sprayed away and was amazed at the resistance of the yellow jackets until I saw that what she had handed me was a can of air freshener.

The kids hid in the room and shoved suitcases out the door one-at-a-time to my wife who then ran them to me at various places in the parking lot. Between suitcases, I would floor the accelerator, pop the clutch and rocket the car to another corner of the parking lot with the hope of eluding the yellow jackets.

The old woman who had lent me the can of air freshener stood by and watched.

"I ain't never seen nuthin' like this," she said.

I hadn't either.

Yellow jackets also made life miserable at the annual arts and crafts show in Bel Air in September. Joining the thousands of people were thousands of yellow jackets. The people were drawn by the water-color paintings, the carved ducks and such. The yellow jackets came for the open-pit beef and the spilled soda on the food tables.

Hundreds of drowned yellow jackets floated in a shallow brown pool of Coca-Cola spilled on the counter at one refreshment stand. It was a miserable day for man and for some yellow jackets, too.

It was around that time that the faculty at my school held an after-school crab feast at Double Rock Park in Parkville. The event was a bit expensive for a family of five and we didn't go. I drove home from school the Friday of the crab feast thinking sadly of all the crabs and camaraderie I was missing.

But on Monday morning I heard that yellow jackets in plague proportion had descended on the crab feast and spread havoc.

The people who had the most fun, as far as I could tell from the stories, were those who had been stung only two or three times. At lunch on Monday, they pointed to the places on their lips and cheeks where they had been stung.

One teacher bragged that the yellow jackets had not bothered his table because he had sprayed everything with bee killer.

The thought of eating steamed crabs lightly coated with bee killer does not appeal to me, and I ended up being happy and thankful that I had not gone to the crab feast.

Yellow jackets live from spring to fall. During the hot months, the purpose of a yellow jacket's life is to gather food for the young and to enlarge the nest to accommodate the growing colony. When autumn comes, the work of the colony is over. The few females who will be the new queens disperse. Only they will survive the winter. Each hibernates in solitude and single-handedly starts a new colony in the spring.

All the other yellow jackets are left like soldiers at the end of the war to wander about without purpose and to live as marauders. In short supply is food. Where is the awful-and-beautiful diet of flies and nectar they thrived on all summer?

So the yellow jackets come and ruin fruit in orchards, ruin picnics and art shows. The yellow jacket will sit on a child's lips to draw the juice of chewing gum and fly into a man's mouth for food. They pester us as the weather turns cold for something to eat before they die.

# FISH STORY

Trout season opened in Harford County on the eve of April Fool's Day. I know the wily trout got a laugh out of that.

It was a cold weekend. Snow was still on the ground in the shadow of the barn at Eden Mill dam on Deer Creek.

The first trout got away because I had disassembled my reel the night before to oil a squeak and I had put the reel back together incorrectly. A rainbow trout went for a hook hidden inside a ball of Velveeta cheese. I pulled the rod to set the hook and the trout broke water and thrashed in the air.

Then the reel malfunctioned and the trout took off downstream through rocks and white water, as line wildly unspooled beyond my control.

"I'll land this one by hand!" I said to the kids. I grabbed the line and threw the rod down on the creek bank.

The two older kids and I had taken up sportfishing just a few weeks before and it was the first fish that we had hooked.

I pulled on the line like Hemingway's Santiago in *The Old Man and the Sea*. I was sure that the experienced anglers wading about in deep boots with all sorts of trout fishing gear strapped to their bodies were impressed with my trout fishing finesse. They fish with the equanimity of English butlers.

But I stood on the bank and pulled away. Yards and yards of spindly plastic line twisted and piled around me until I looked like a man who had been involved in an explosion in a spaghetti factory. Then, just when I got the trout to the edge of the bank, it leapt in the air and threw the hook.

After waiting a few minutes for me to spend my wrath, a friendly angler from Pennsylvania waded downstream to investigate the admirable disorder I had created on the bank. He pulled a tool kit from an olive-drab pocket and fixed my reel in five minutes. As he worked, I told him of how I had spent an hour the night before taking the reel apart down to the last hair-thin washer, only to find that the squeak wasn't inside the reel. It was in the little plastic knob on the crank and could have been fixed in one second with one drop of oil without taking anything apart. Then I told him that this was the first fish I had ever hooked.

"I can believe it," he said.

How the line got back on the reel is an untellable story as long as the line itself.

I then hooked a second trout which fought like a bootful of water with a life of its own.

"Get the net! Get the net!" I called above the roar of the water to the kids.

At that moment, feeling the pull of the fish, I wished that they, too, could hook a trout so they could know how magnificent it feels.

"You forgot the net! You forgot the net!" the kids called back.

"Get the bucket! Get the bucket!" I yelled.

I had bought a large plastic pail for bringing home fish.

They brought the bucket. Then a scene unfolded on the bank of Deer Creek that must have looked to all around like we were trying to beat the trout to death with a bucket. Probably reluctant to surrender in such a humiliating circumstance, the trout threw himself into the air with many twists like a circus performer and set himself free.

Ever since the fishing bug bit us, we have been watching all the fishing shows on cable TV. Fishing shows have a simple format: Guys with boats worth more than my house catch fish one after another for 30 minutes. It's like watching news highlights of a ball game which make nine innings look like a machine gun burst of home runs and great catches.

We have also taken to spending time in the fishing gear areas of department stores. We browse and ask questions of everyone we meet. "I've been fishing all my life," an old man warned us, "and I figure that every fish I've ever caught cost me a hundred dollars." That depressed us, but then another guy told us the story of the 80 crappies he had caught the day before. That was when we went to the housewares department and bought the big bucket.

We have caught no fish so far, but we will not give up. All of our trips end with the loading of the car for the long trip home. The last item to go in the trunk is always the bucket as big as our dreams, filled with reality and a few crumpled lunch bags.

# BREATHLESS

The free instruction booklet I sent for with a coupon that came with my new harmonica carries no warning that if you are taking up harmonica playing beyond the prime of life you may hyperventilate and fall out of your chair.

It should.

A warning in the booklet cautions against playing with gum or candy in your mouth, but there is no warning about older people keeling over.

What surprises me most about the harmonica is that down to the last detail I can recall, it seems identical to the one my father has had for about 50 years. Even the box with its curved cardboard lid and paper hinge seem the same. He played harmonica as a kid in Patterson Park on the Bank Street hill on summer nights with his friends. Someone had a ukulele and they often drew small crowds as the gas street lights were lit by men walking beats. When I was a kid he would get out his harmonica now and then and play a little.

Between spit-and-squeak practice sessions I have been working on completing a number of applications for educational summer programs for teachers. But I find myself reluctant to include --when the forms ask about hobbies and interests-- any mention of the harmonica. I can imagine the chairman of a summer institute shuffling through applications before an admissions panel: "Let's see now. Here we have a chap who can play 'Hot Cross Buns' on the harmonica."

"Hot Cross Buns" is the first tune you are taught in the booklet; it is followed by "Mary Had a Little Lamb," which is also the tune to the Merrily-we-roll-along part of "Good Night Ladies." After that you learn the "Alphabet Song," which has the same tune as "Twinkle, Twinkle Little Star" and "Baa Baa Black Sheep."

By learning only three tunes you can have a six-piece repertoire. This, I imagine, is encouraging to a beginner who may have visions of taking requests from his stool at the pub as billiard balls click in the background. "Hey, pal," someone surely will call, "do you know 'Baa Baa Black Sheep'?"

Each song in the booklet has a brief Lawrence Welk-type introduction: "Here is another little tune, known all the world over and ending with those popular words, 'My fair lady,' " ("London Bridge Is Falling Down"); "And now one of the great songs of all time, that should be played and sung in every home" ("Home Sweet Home"). I guess you are supposed to memorize this stuff in case you ever get good enough to play at parties and you need a little snappy patter between tunes.

Some songs, though, are meant for the harmonica and I think that most people would agree that "Home Sweet Home" is one of them. I have been trying to learn how to play it. It makes the kitchen sound like the bunkhouse in an old cowboy movie.

Although harmonica playing may not be regarded as very sophisticated, three U.S. presidents, according to the booklet from Hohner, Inc., were "harmonica-people" -- Abraham Lincoln, Calvin Coolidge and Dwight D. Eisenhower.

I can see Honest Abe at his desk with harmonica in hand, adjusting his glasses, leaning forward and studying the numbered notes and little inhale-exhale arrows on a free how-to-play-the-harmonica paper. I can see Cool Cal leaning back, dreaming of the Vermont hills and harpin' "Home Sweet Home" as he tapped his foot on the polished boards of the White House floor. I can see Ike at his Gettysburg farm saying, "Here's one for ya, Mamie," and blowing a few bars of "Skip to My Lou."

So maybe I am in good company.

Being a harmonica-person is serious business, apparently. Along with the instruction booklet came a brochure of items that only a harmonica-person could love. Items include a cap with a *Keep on Harpin'* patch; a shirt stamped with a large harmonica with *Easy Reeding* printed above it; a twenty-dollar necklace with a gold-plated harmonica pendant. And there's much more in the manner of coffee mugs and beach bags --all stamped with harmonicas. They even offer a two foot-long, six inch-high ornamental harmonica. I am not sure what harmonica-people do with them.

An odd thing about playing the harmonica is that after a long session your mouth is left hanging freely open with your lips stretched involuntarily over your teeth. I find myself walking around the house like Mr. Before in an old-time (Do you have to gum your mush?) dental ad.

But, at least, I am both smiling and breathless. Which, as time passes, is not often an easy trick.

# OWL STORY

I have been trying to file papers and clean my desk, an annual summer rite I skipped last year. But it is not going well because none of the papers seem related.

Nevertheless, I am setting up a system using manila folders, naming all files "Items of Interest" and numbering them to tell them apart. I have completed two so far.

"Items of Interest-1" contains a filing card with a good title for a novel, a hand-drawn map to Bruce Springsteen's house in Rumson, N.J., a page of notes about a funeral service and a few notes I have just written about tennis balls.

The novel title is *Owls for Supper*. My children developed it during a brainstorming session designed to catapult me to literary fame and deposit them into designer clothes. They thought if I started with a good title, a good novel would follow easily.

"So, what will the story be about?" I asked.

"Well," said one, "It's a sad story about a poor family that has to eat owls."

"No," said another, "It's a happy story about a goofy family that eats owls and does other crazy things, but everyone in the village loves them because they are happy even though they eat owls."

This story line had some appeal.

The third child said, "It's the story of a man named Supper who needs owls and has to work hard against impossible odds to get owls."

I didn't ask why Supper needed owls, or why he was called Supper. A novel is too much typing, anyway.

The map to Bruce Springsteen's house was drawn by my wife's young cousin during a recent family reunion in Rumson. Since I had heard Bruce lived a few blocks away, I hated to leave without stopping by. I really couldn't admit to my wife and kids that I was stopping intentionally: "I have to stop and check the oil." I said. "And look! We're right in front of Bruce Springsteen's house! And our car tires are crunching the gravel of his driveway! What a surprise!"

The drive is chained off, though I wouldn't have entered anyway (there are limits), and we stopped to get a glimpse of the house through the trees. I had expected people on the lawn cavorting to wild music, but all we saw was a squirrel. A jeep and station wagon were parked before the stately house.

Notes on the funeral service record how many people, myself included, mistook a tape recorder on a pedestal beside the minister for a container of the deceased's ashes. Mark Twain could have produced a chapter on this misunderstanding. Even the widow was amused.

My notes on tennis balls are about the unbelievable change at stuffy Wimbledon permitting the use of yellow balls instead of traditional white balls, which were almost invisible on television. TV commentators mention that the balls are yellow at least once a minute, and I am sure we except color changes in many other traditional items.

"Items of Interest-2" contains a scrap of paper with the names of three models on "The Price is Right" (Janice, Diane, Holly), a recent Harford County newspaper story on the life of a 99-year-old man, a filing card dated May 8, 1985 with notes on Channel 11's extensive coverage of a cat stuck on a ledge and a recipe booklet for artificial crab legs.

It is hard work, but there is a satisfaction that comes from finally getting organized.

# SEASONS IN MARKED BOXES

# A WORLD OF UNEQUATABLE THINGS

Like Indian corn and pumpkins, I think of orange and black jellybeans as fruits of the season. Or, at least, fruits of Halloween week.

Many people eat orange and black jellybeans every year during this week. I do not consciously choose to eat them. It seems to be more a blind response to some instinct.

It is similar to my need to eat corn on the cob on the Fourth of July, to eat celery stalks before Thanksgiving dinner, to take a glass of sherry on Christmas Eve. Man, quite obviously, is not as free as he thinks.

But people who eat orange and black jellybeans during Halloween week do not worry too much about fate and free will. They tend to be simple people with blurred dots of orange and black on the insides of their hands.

Their breath smells like Halloween.

They do not let anyone see their palms when they sit at a table at an important meeting because what they say might not be thought important if they have colored dots on their hands.

I am sure that my seasonal appetite for orange and black jellybeans, which I now regard as instinctive, is, more than likely, nothing more than learned behavior.

The teachers at a grammar school on Gorsuch Avenue near Memorial Stadium used to give orange and black jellybeans to children during Halloween week. If you did a good job of coloring a picture of witches at a cauldron or of a pile of pumpkins with your orange and black crayons, you got a few orange and black jellybeans plunked down on your desk. Everything was orange and black during Halloween week.

My greatest disappointment at that time was that orange and black crayons didn't smell like orange and black jellybeans.

Good old Binney and Smith crayons --which were probably used to sign the Mayflower Compact-- still smell like hot, well-oiled shafts of three-horsepower furnace-blower motors.

It was good to sit in the warm room, to eat jellybeans and color witches black and pumpkins orange. It was all very simple. There were no quadratic equations, no dangling modifiers. It was a world full of dangles and unequatable things.

Our mouths were fed with jellybeans and our eyes were fed with pictures. Stories were put into our ears. The senses mixed: Witches must surely smell and taste like licorice, pumpkins like great sweet-jelly oranges. We put yellow into the eyes and mouths of jack o'lanterns.

In the corners of our pictures of witches, we drew black spider webs. They looked like fragments of mesh stockings. The smart girl whose father had a white-collar job put red in the eye of a black cat and got an extra jellybean. I made a mental note of that for the next year. It was a good idea. When we colored during Halloween week, the room smelled of licorice and electric motors.

The kids have been bringing Halloween papers home from their school. Recent third-grade homework included the writing of a ghost story. The special paper they were given to write on had a drawing of a ghost at the top.

Parents have to sign homework papers. The story I signed was about a girl in a "deserted, spooky, peculiar house." It was a good story which gave darkness a shape by explaining a mystery.

Darkness lost its shape in the kindergarten painting that was brought home.

"Too much black paint got on the cat and he's hard to see." That was the explanation of the field of black.

But the pumpkin was a good orange pumpkin. You could tell it was a pumpkin.

I sniffed at a witch picture colored with crayon to see if I could smell licorice. No licorice, just hot motors. Nothing has changed.

On Halloween night, I will ceremoniously light the many jack o'lanterns we set about the front yard every year. Parents will be out with flashlights and the neighborhood will swap candy with itself. There will be plenty of packets of orange and black jellybeans among the booty that will be taken.

The children keep the past from disappearing. It is a kind of trick and mystery.

# THE EYES OF PLIMOTH

Gone from the center of the dining room table is the ceramic jack o'lantern. In its place now stand two figurines, a Pilgrim man and Pilgrim woman. The table is set for November.

For years, I have eaten my November meals while looking at the neatly dressed, porcelain-bright Pilgrim couple. But they do not bear much resemblance to the starved, ragged lot described in Governor William Bradford's journal, "Of Plimoth Plantation."

It is just as well, perhaps, I do not think I could eat my month's worth of broiled fish, rare roast beef and buttered vegetables with two gaunt, half-naked wretches staring back at me.

The bric-a-brac masters of Hong Kong know how to make a buck by feeding our dreams.

The Pilgrim man who sits on the table has a long gray beard. He is tall, dignified and old --the way you would expect a founding father to look. But, in fact, only four of the 102 *Mayflower* passengers were over 50 years old. Our forefathers were in their twenties and thirties.

That famous couple which poet Longfellow later romanticized, John Alden and Priscilla Mullins, were but 21 and 18. Miles Standish, the army of one at Plymouth Plantation, was 36 and far from forefather-tall. He was so short that he was called Captain Shrimp behind his back. The first governor, John Carver, who died at the end of the first winter at the age of 54, was replaced by William Bradford, age 31.

Bradford was elected as he lay ill in a hut made of twigs and mud, which gives you some idea of the shape these people were in. He recovered, though, and governed for 33 years.

The face on the figurine of the Pilgrim woman on the dining room table is sedate. Her cheeks are colored with pale pink paint. She is tall with pride and her apron is stiff and white. She does not look like one of the 29 women who lived between decks on the *Mayflower*, which was packed like a latter-day slaver. She does not look like she had consumed little else than beer (it kept better than water) and salted fish three times a day during four months at sea.

The actual crossing took two months, but the Pilgrims spent two additional months at sea because they had to turn back to England twice due to leaks in their companion ship, the *Speedwell*, which they eventually left behind.

No, the serene face on the figurine is not the face of Dorothy Bradford, wife of William Bradford, who spent four months at sea to come to a wilderness that offered no solace. Within a month of dropping anchor, while still living on the ship, Dorothy Bradford, her clothing filthy and hard with frozen brine, threw herself despairingly from the *Mayflower* into the bay at Cape Cod. She was 23 years old.

Although the porcelain figures in the center of the table appear too old here and too healthy there, their bearing is proud. And this pride was real.

Ten years after his wife jumped to her death at what seemed to be the dead end of the world, William Bradford began to write his famous journal which recorded the history of the Pilgrims. In describing their arrival in America, he was almost sinfully proud. America was the new Canaan. He was Moses. And the Pilgrims who had fled from England to Holland and then to the New World were the Israelites who had wandered in the desert before reaching the Promised Land.

Bradford felt no shame in pointing out that the Pilgrims had crossed the "mighty ocean," though "wise Seneca" had fallen sick when sailing but a few miles off the coast of Italy; that they faced "salvages" who were ready to "fill their sids full of arrows" and a "countrie full of woods and thickets" and of "wild and salvage hiew," whereas St. Paul had been welcomed by the inhabitants of Malta where his gospel ship wrecked. Bradford boasted that they had not even the mountain Moses had, a Pisgah, from which they might take hope by viewing from the wilderness a land of milk and honey.

Bradford was overwhelmed with pride: "May not & ought not the children of these fathers, rightly say: 'Our fathers were Englishmen which came over this great ocean, and were ready to perish in this wilderness.' "

And perish they did that first winter.

The two little figures will sit silently among my eggs, ales and steaks during this month of plenty that will culminate with turkey and pie. Do they remember their children crying with hunger? The sound of the empty Atlantic? Do they see the graves they leveled and left unmarked to hide their thinning number from the Indians? I know their eyes are dots of black paint, but I sometimes think they are watching me.

# SIDE BY SIDE

I have always been fascinated by paintings that feature juxtapositions, such as William Glacken's "Nude with Apple" and Edouard Manet's "Woman with a Parrot." Such paintings make you wonder about alternatives. For instance: What if the nude were holding a fish sandwich? What if the woman standing by the perched parrot were standing by a circus elephant or a large wheel of gouda cheese?

A more imaginative form of juxtaposition is the metaphorical association of an art work's title and its content. Morton Schamberg's sculpture "God," for example, is a few pieces of interconnected plumbing fittings rising from a carpenter's miter box. The piece, a product of the Dada movement early in the century, was meant to be shocking and anti-social. But I find Schamberg's "God," apart from historical interpretation, a reverential wonderment.

The miter box evokes an image of Joseph the carpenter and --though there is no biblical Pete the plumber-- the convoluted plumbing suggests the dynamism and mystery of God. The viewer is left to wonder: Is this all of God? Or a part --just one synapse, perhaps-- of God? And how does God work?

Someday this piece of sculpture could replace the world's accumulation of religious symbols.

But the most intriguing type of juxtaposition is of what is depicted in a painting and what is suggested beyond the frame of the painting. An appropriate example as Thanksgiving approaches is G. H. Broughton's "Pilgrims Going to Church." It is a narrow rectangular painting of the advance portion of a column of pilgrims marching through a snowy forest toward a shed-like church.

All the men, with the exception of the clergyman, carry guns. Two men leading the column appear to be conversing easily. The cleric follows with his eyes cast down in thought; his wife has her nose just a bit in the air.

The next person is the central figure. She is a radiant young woman who reminds me of a statue of a madonna fitted out in clothing, such as I have seen in some churches in old neighborhoods. Unlike the other figures, she seems to be standing still and appears about to be trampled by a swarthy fellow wearing a soldier's helmet. The color of her clothing is lighter than that worn by any of the others and with her small daughter in hand, they appear to be an American version of madonna-and-child.

Behind her is the dark soldier and a stern-looking woman in a tall hat. Next is a woman carrying an infant, accompanied by a young boy with his head held high and a teenage daughter who seems to be looking toward the church with apprehension. She knows, I imagine, that she is going to have to endure a two-hour harangue about hell and sin.

Following are two men who have stopped suddenly.

The younger of the two looks keenly toward us into the forest beyond the frame of the picture. He puts a hand back toward his companion to have him halt and hush. Has he seen something or heard something? A little detective work indicates that something was heard (rather than seen) because the child of the madonna, ahead in line, has turned and she is looking over her shoulder toward where the alert young man is looking. Only two figures have heard something in the forest.

And what happened next is for us to wonder.

It was a violent time, as evidenced by a passage from Governor Bradford's journal describing an attack by the settlers in 1637 on an Indian fortification:

"Those that first entered found sharp resistance from the enemie, who both shot at & grapled with them; others rane into their howses, & brought out fire, and sett them on fire...With the wind, all was quickly on a flame, and thereby more were burnte to death than was otherwise slain...Those that scaped the fire were slaine with the sword: some hewed to peeces, others run through with their rapiers...It was conceived that they thus destroyed 400 at this time. It was a fearful sight to see them thus frying in the fryer, and the strems of blood quenching the same, and horrible was the stinck & sente ther of; but the victory seemed a sweet sacrifice, and they gave the prays ther of to God."

I, myself, think that the pilgrims in the painting made it safely to church without incident. I can imagine them in the dim building in the wilderness as night fell and they worshipped and gave thanks for all the Indians they had ever torched and "hewed." Never entertaining even once the thought that their God could look like a spare part for the Millennium Falcon. Or that they could do wrong.

But it is not fair for me to judge the pilgrims. Their world was hard and feral. My world is comfortable. And I have little more with which to concern myself than an apple in the hand of a nude, and a parrot that just doesn't look right.

# CHRISTMAS ON THE ROAD

Two dominant themes in Christmas songs and stories are being home for the holidays and not being home for the holidays.

Through the efforts of such as Charles Dickens and Bing Crosby, these simple and emotional leitmotifs have been entrenched to an archetypal depth.

But are there any songs, any stories, for those who are neither home nor not-home on Christmas? Every other year, my wife's side of the family gathers in New Jersey on Christmas Day. This means we have to spend half of Christmas traveling on the Kennedy Highway, the New Jersey Turnpike, and an hour's worth of two-lane roads that wind into the marshes of Rumson. Is there a Bing to sing for those who spend Christmas Day on the road?

I went to the large record store in the shopping mall. Because country music has a reputation for having a song to cover the emotions of every human experience, I went immediately to the country music section.

There I found a bin of holiday records marked: *I'll Be Home for Christmas*. Next to it was another bin marked: *I Won't Be Home for Christmas*. I asked the man who was stocking the bins if there were any *I'll Be In Between* records. "There might be something in the *I Won't Be Home* bin," he said.

I started flipping through the records. I knew I would probably find an album with a picture of a trucker alone in the cab of his rig with a little Fuller-brush Christmas tree on the seat beside him. The album would probably be called, "Don't Pull that Cork on the Wassail Bowl till I Bring this Big Rig Home, Momma."

But I flipped and flipped, and there was nothing. The closest I came was a song called, "I'm Eating Truckstop Turkey, Momma." Momma, a musical genre akin to the blues, is popular with truckers and Freudians; but it's not sufficiently sentimental for my taste.

I left empty-handed as shoppers who would be home and shoppers who would not be home filled their arms with record albums. I turned and, with eyes on the floor, walked away.

The year before last, we spent a gray Christmas Day driving to Rumson and a cold black night driving back. We will do it again this year. Leaving Rumson on Christmas night requires driving past many houses with smoking chimneys and with dark windows blinking with colored Christmas lights. The desire to stop the car, slip inside one of the cozy-looking houses, and go to sleep is overwhelming.

I have no one to blame but myself for spending every other Christmas on the road. A month after my wife and I were engaged, she warned me of her family's salmon-like urge to go to Rumson every two years on Christmas day.

After that first Christmas in Rumson, a day of showing-off the smallest diamond ring which Kirk's in Baltimore had to sell, we entered the twilight zone of the New Jersey Turnpike. At one of the several Howard Johnson's at which we paused on the return trip, the waitress, a college girl, placed the paper mats, the knives, forks and spoons; then she filled the water glasses and asked for our order. Abashed by all the attention, I said, "I'm sorry; we only want two cups of tea."

"Sorry? What do you mean, *sorry*?" she said. "You want tea, right? You have a right to ask for tea. You should just come in and say, 'I want some tea,' right?" Her counter companion, an old waitress with sternly folded leg-of-mutton arms, shook her head. I avoided her glance.

"I guess you are right," I said to the young girl. I was too tired to care. After all, she was spending Christmas on the New Jersey Turnpike, too. This is just one example of what Christmas on the road is like. But I learned my lesson. Now I always burst through the doors of every fast-food restaurant I encounter on the New Jersey Turnpike on Christmas and in an imperious tone demand hot tea, milk for the kids, and a booth in which to change the latest baby's diaper.

Even though there is no Christmas song for me, I have decided to make the best of this year's trip to Rumson. Surely, the true spirit of Christmas is traveling: It's 90 miles from Nazareth to Bethlehem, and the trip took four days by donkey and foot 2,000 years ago.

At least one book has a story for me.

# UNPACKING CHRISTMAS

Somewhat mechanical--that's how the coming of Christmas felt the other day as I pulled boxes marked *Pre-Christmas* from the shelf.

The boxes marked *Summer* on the shelves along the back wall of the basement have finally quieted down. The crabs have stopped rapping against the cardboard in their arcane marine code. Only a faint tidal lap comes from the box marked *Ocean City*, though it smells strongly of creosote and popcorn, yet.

When I was a bachelor, I was sloppy with my seasons. My tinsel and my plastic pumpkins were all mixed-up with my pencils and magazines. I kept Valentine hearts in the cabinet with the cups. You couldn't walk from the front door to the kitchen without stepping on four-leaf clovers, Easter eggs and mistletoe.

Now, thanks to my wife, all the seasons and holidays are packed in marked boxes that cover the back wall of the basement from floor to ceiling. Time moves as boxes are alternately pulled and replaced from left to right and top to bottom. It is a kind of real calendar.

As I pulled the *Pre-Christmas* boxes the other night, the kids took turns climbing the step-ladder to listen to the squirrels foraging for acorns inside one of the *Autumn* boxes I had just packed and sealed with wet strips of brown paper tape.

Then they gathered around as I slit the tape on a *Pre-Christmas* box. Red candles, a handful of thin ones and a fat one, came out to replace the orange ones that had just been packed away with the squirrels.

The wooden stable I made many years ago came out next. But for a layer of straw and some little hand-carved animals, it will sit empty on top of the piano until Christmas.

We unrolled the Advent calendar my wife made. On the roll of heavy material is a felt Christmas tree. Under the tree are 25 pockets which contain intricately fashioned felt ornaments that are put on the tree one-a-day until Christmas.

The kids heard the rustling in the box marked *Winter: Yard Birds* first. I carried it upstairs to the back door and turned them loose in the sun and cold air. Cow birds, starlings, blue jays, the fiery cardinal and his mate --they dropped their shadows onto the porch and flew toward the sun.

The trains were pulled from another box and the kids began unwrapping the sand houses that will sit over colored lights on the train platform. The houses are made of cardboard. They were covered with glue, dipped into coarse sand, painted --and, while the paint was still wet, dipped into fine, white sand for a gum-drop effect.

Little by little, week after week, Christmas will be unpacked. Caravans bearing pine cones, ribbons, ornaments, window candles, statues of Santa Claus and Frosty will ascend the basement stairs and return for more.

The idea of "unpacking" Christmas makes me feel like a stagehand in a theater, or a window dresser in a department store. My wife suggests that I think of it as "unfolding" Christmas.

She has the right idea, I suppose, but I can't help getting a little humbuggy about the abundance of Christmas stuff we have and the thought that what takes weeks and weeks to unpack and carry upstairs will all be carried back down and repacked on that one day when we feel like we have finally had enough of Christmas.

I cheated a little and let the kids peek into one of the boxes marked *Christmas*.

As I slit the tape, the air that came from inside the box was cold. We all felt it. It was dark inside the box. It was hard to see until our eyes adjusted to seeing by starlight. The box was filled with sandy hills and foreign looking trees with twisted trunks. On one hillside, at the mouth of a cave, we saw a small fire. Several men were sitting by the fire.

"We hear flute music," the kids said.

"That's enough for now," I said as I folded the lid. "The time for this box will come."

That is one box I have never minded unpacking. But I have always felt a bit guilty at the end of Christmas, on the day when we have had enough of it, that I pack it up along with the candles and colored lights and shelve it till next year.

# AN INCH, AND MANY MILES

I always enjoy talking to people who wear eyeglasses when they are standing by a Christmas tree.

Often, when they are fixed in just the right place, their eyes disappear. They are replaced with two twin Christmas trees. Each eye becomes a curious bowl of electrically colored jujubes.

I once talked to a bespectacled young woman who was wearing a sheer dress and a yard of blonde hair as she stood by a Christmas tree. But she did not seem very sexy as she spoke with me because she had a Christmas tree in each eye.

At another holiday gathering, a Scrooge type who wore glasses never knew that he had blinking flying-saucer eyes as he sat before the Christmas tree. His glassy mask made him Christmasfied whether he liked it or not.

I first discovered this simple eyeglass phenomenon as a little child at my grandmother's house. Once, when I was sitting by the Christmas tree near the generous front window that opened all the house to any passerby on the street, my great-aunt, who lived just up the block from my grandmother, leaned forward in her chair to talk to me. I was startled to see that she had Christmas trees in her eyes. A Christmas tree was also in the front window glass and I felt surrounded, pleasantly, by colored lights.

Even back then, her lenses were very thick. She asked me if I had been a good boy and I lied and said, "Yes." She asked if Santa Claus had come to my house and I told the truth and said, "Yes."

It is hard for great-aunts and little children to have really good conversations.

She did not have children, which was unusual in a family that seemed to sneeze children. There were so many children and grandchildren that the family had to eat in shifts, many shifts throughout the afternoon and evening. A browned turkey or ham was always being carved. There was no place in the house where a person could get far enough away to fit everyone in a snapshot. Almost every year, someone tried to do it. People from the neighborhood who passed by would tap on the front window and wave Merry Christmas to us. They would not come in because there was no room.

Then my grandmother died and it was all over. The gravitational center was gone.

Through the years, my great-aunt's glasses have become thicker and thicker. Hospital operations did not work very well. The last time I saw her, she really couldn't see much, but she still wore her glasses. I noticed that everything she couldn't see was just an inch away from her shining on the front of her glasses.

But it is an inch that will not be breached.

That was 10 years ago at Christmas. I had my first real conversation with her then. I sat in her kitchen and asked about what she remembered of Germany where she was born a decade before the turn of the century. She could not remember too well, she said, but she did recall that once a priest had asked her to pick some onions for him. That was just before she came to America.

Her house is mostly dark these days because she does not need to turn lights on anymore. And the family does not come back to the old street the way it used to.

I was reminded of that Christmas of 30 years ago by the middle child who saw colored lights in my eyeglasses the other night when I put up the Christmas tree. He is very much involved with the holiday this year. He pulled the tree off the porch, through the door and into the family room all by himself. He was anxious for me to put it up; I put it up.

He is about as old as I was when I first discovered Christmas eyeglasses. After the tree was up and I had strung the lights, the others went back to the living room to watch TV. The decorations only come on Christmas Eve. I sat with the middle child in the darkened room after the others had gone. He saw the tree "two times" in my glasses.

I felt strange knowing that he could look into my eyes and see what I could not see.

I thought of my great-aunt and her eyeglasses that night and of the 10 years that had passed since my last visit. I realize that it was more than a Christmas tree two-times that I could not see.

# SAY IT WITH A CROCK

The origin of the holiday custom of sending people sausages and cheeses through mail-order houses can be traced to the first decade A.D. in the Middle East.

"Look what arrived today from the three wise men," she said.

"Aren't they coming to visit?" he asked as he brushed sawdust from his arms.

"Not this year," she said. "Caspar sent *Smokehouse Gang,* an 'excellent sausage assortment from the heart of Wisconsin's sausage country.' Balthazar sent *Barrel-O-Pistachios,* a wood-grain polystyrene barrel 'chockful of munchy flavorful enjoyment.' "

"What about Melchior? What did he send?"

"*Cheese Chalet,* 'fabulous flavor favorites to get the holidays off to a great start.' "

"A great finish, I think," he said.

My cheese-and-sausage gift catalog from last year was still sitting on my desk when the new edition arrived. I hadn't ordered anything last year, but I guess the company has some sort of faith in me.

Most prices have risen a little. Last year, gift 202, the *Personalized Crock* (of cheese) was $6.95; this year it costs $7.50 for a personalized crock. Gift 189, 10 feet of rope sausage, is up a dollar. But in the candy section, the price of *Dietetic Jubilee,* a "variety show of sugarless delights," held at $11.95. Nothing got cheaper.

It is not really odd that I still have last year's catalog. I retained the booklet for my library because it is a form of imaginative literature, I think, on the generally uncelebrated subject of cheese and sausage. Good prose about a pound of braunschweiger is hard to come by.

Here is the beginning of a paragraph about six micro-wheels of cheese called *Gourmet Favorites:* "Bored with Brick? Tired of Tilsit? Even a bit ho hum about Cheddar? Here's the gift to set your tastebuds dancing."

The advertising copy writer, a kind of modern poet, has outdone himself here. "Bored with Brick? Tired of Tilsit?" is a fine example of parallel phrasing and alliteration.

The "Tired of Tilsit?" spunkily intimidates the average Velveeta-class reader. "What's Tilsit?" he wonders. The writer's stroke is subtle and the reader infers that *Gourmet Favorites* really must be gourmet cheese if it's for people who are tired of something he never heard of. (When I surveyed some associates to see if they knew what Tilsit was, the closest answer came from a woman who said it was a kind of wrench used to fix cars.)

The closing image of "tastebuds dancing" is, of course, a lively literary personification. The reader can actually feel effervescent activity on the tongue as tastebuds suffering from cheese ennui kick off their shoes and get ready to dance in anticipation of *Gourmet Favorites*.

I have no Honk-if-you-are-tired-of-Tilsit friends, so I turned the page.

I like to look at the pictures. The dried-fruit trays glisten; the gingerbread house looks cozy. The most boring item in the catalog is a tin of pretzels of the sort I have bought all year long at the supermarket for a lot less money. Then again, at the supermarket you don't get the tin with the nostalgic horse-and-carriage pictures.

The appeal of such catalogs is that you can dispose of shopping and gift-giving anxieties in a flash. And I am tempted: The *VIP Cheddar*, perhaps, for my wife; *Sausage Buffet* for the girl; *Turkey 'n Treats* for the boys to split; a hunk of Tilsit for myself so I can get tired of it.

All you have to do is fill out the form and write a check. Slam-bang-Merry Christmas it's done.

But that's not what these catalog items are for, I guess. I really don't have the heart to send my 3-year-old a personalized crock. I know I don't have the courage to send my wife *Snack Basket*. Such gifts are for business men to send each other. They are for old friends who live far apart to send.

The gears of business can be greased with cheese. And old friends can be drawn close with links of sausage.

# BEARINGS

There's an outfit in Blacksburg, Virginia, that will send you a freshly cut mail-order Christmas tree via UPS. But that's not for me.

Before we went to cut down our own Christmas tree, I went out to the car to get the map of Harford County. I had several clippings of advertisements from nurseries and Christmas tree farms. I was trying to figure out which was the one we had gone to last year.

We wanted to return there, but we have been to many Christmas tree farms in Harford County in the years we have lived here and all the small country roads and tree-cutting memories are jumbled.

Even the map is a bit of a mess. So many routes have been highlighted with a yellow marker that the purpose of highlighting has been defeated. Our neighborhood sits on the map in the midst of a great yellow web.

I traced one highlighted route northwest and tapped my finger. "I think this is where we went last year," I said to my wife.

She looked at the map. "No, that's the way to the kids' dentist's new office."

"Hmm," I said. Hmm is what I always say when I look at maps.

"Then maybe this is the way," I said as I ran my finger northeast along another yellow road.

"No," she said. "That's the way to the fishing spot you never did find."

I finally decided that where we had gone last year was toward the northwest far past the kids' dentist's new office. I figured we had to turn left north of the dentist's office onto the highlighted road that ran to the doctor's house. We would go past the doctor's house for quite a bit until we got to a little luncheonette in the middle of nowhere where my wife once had a terrible sandwich when she was driving kids around the county for the traveling soccer league. Then, when we got to the luncheonette, we would turn right and go north for a distance which we learned last year is longer than you think.

I resolved that we would not turn off the road too soon by the house that is painted the wrong color for the neighborhood and get lost for a half-hour like last year. I folded the map with confidence. I knew exactly where I was going.

And I did.

We ticked off the landmarks as we drove along. "There's where our dentist is!" the kids said as we passed a very unmedical-looking building sitting by itself on the edge of a ridge that fell away into a pasture. Then we passed the doctor's house. We know where the doctor lives because he will see you at his house on Sunday if you are really sick. The last time we were there, he conducted the examination in his living room as his family ate breakfast in the kitchen.

A touch of the country way of life can be found in Harford County, but you do need a map and a sense of direction to get around because everything is kind of spread out.

"There's where Mommy got the bad sandwich but the pizza was OK!" the kids said as they looked ahead.

I checked the map. "Hmm," I said. The kids were correct. We were approaching the luncheonette in the middle of nowhere where I planned to turn right. At the luncheonette, we turned and headed north on the road that is longer than you think. We passed the house that is painted the wrong color for the neighborhood without yielding to the temptation to turn off like we did last year, and we arrived at the Christmas tree farm without getting lost.

I took the saw from the trunk. "Is that the saw that got stuck in the tree last year?" everyone asked.

"Yes," I said.

We headed for the hill that we climbed last year when it was snowing and the trail was icy. We decided last year that the hill really was too hard to climb after we got to the top. Armed with the saw that got stuck in the tree, we again climbed the hill that is too hard to climb and headed for the trees that were farthest away. The best trees are always farthest away.

Last year we got a tree that was too tall for the living room and this year we managed to find another one just like it. Trees in the wild always seem to look shorter than they really are.

Returning to the base of the hill that is too hard to climb, we were charged more than the tree was worth by the man at the tent. It was exactly what he had charged us last year.

I tossed the saw that got stuck in the tree again into the trunk and tied the tree that was too tall for the living room again onto the roof of the car that is really too small to haul a Christmas tree. I tied it to the car in such a clever way that none of the windows could be fully closed for the trip home.

I suppose I could buy a mail-order Christmas tree and wait at home until the tree rings the doorbell. But it's more fun to get out in the country on a winter day and drag a tree down a hill the way people do in pictures on Christmas cards.

I checked the map as we left the tree farm, but we ended up on what we now call the road that doesn't look right. Nevertheless, we were headed home. Which always is somewhere down the line.

# WALDEN'S OTHER CHAPTER

I was standing on a stepladder in the backyard trying to lasso the top of a 14-foot Norway spruce when a chickadee flew up and perched on the nub at the whip-like top of the tree. To be a bird!, I thought as I made another adjustment to the lariat knot in the length of clothesline.

School children can be thankful that this did not happen to Thoreau, since it would have moved him to lengthen *Walden* by another chapter. I was glad that this had not happened to Thoreau, because it would be very hard assuring youngsters that there is significance in a chickadee sitting atop a Christmas tree. Although there probably is.

Birds aside, I was trying to lasso the top of the tree with the plan of catching it and pulling the supple upper part of it toward me so I could attach a light at the very top. My wife had got the lights up to about the 12-foot level by throwing the strings of lights up and over branches. But I wanted a light at the very top.

Hoppy and Cisco would not have been impressed with my technique. But after a lot of throws, the idea worked. Finally, when I let go of the tip of the tree, a single white light, the only white light among all the multicolored lights already on the tree, sprang up into its proper place.

The tree in the yard is easier to deal with than the tree that gets dragged into the house.

What's nice about the spruce in the backyard is that it stands straight and won't tip over. It seems that once a Christmas tree is cut down, it never can be made to stand straight again. And if you think you have finally got the tree in the living room straight, it will only look straight from one angle. I usually adjust the tree so it will look straight to people as they come in the front door. First impressions count.

Few Christmas trees worth their tinsel have ever risen to blazing grandeur in anything less than a welter of sailor's blessings. Even people who ordinarily do not swear are moved by a Christmas tree to swearing. I am surprised that the Christmas tree industry hasn't come up with a way of balancing Christmas trees similar to the way tires are balanced. I think I would be willing to pay a few extra dollars to have my Christmas tree balanced.

Last year the tree fell over twice while I was trying to put it up. On the first fall, the tree swept away everything on the coffee table. A painted toucan and an armadillo of red clay shot along the waxed wood and took flight over the edge. Only the armadillo lived. On the second fall, the top of the piano was cleared of portraits and bric-a-brac.

I grabbed the tree by a branch.

"Dad's fighting with the Christmas tree!" the kids screamed as they ran for their mother.

But all the lassoing and tree-fighting seem worth it once the trees are lit and night comes.

I have never liked Christmas trees with all white lights. They look to me like "decorator" Christmas trees. They seem clever and sterile. But most strings of lights come in an old-fashioned assortment of red, blue, green and yellow.

To understand the attraction of color, I read in a book by Max Luscher, the German color-psychologist. It seems that red, blue, green and yellow, having the greatest universal appeal, are considered psychological primaries and that color generally affects us below the level of awareness.

I guess this makes a multicolored Christmas tree a psychological playground for memories and half-thoughts: A path into a forest lit by a green bulb may be explored; then we may wander into the tree through a blue cave; and so on. "The woods are lovely, dark and deep," wrote Robert Frost.

We do seem to have an atavistic urge to disappear into the forest of a Christmas tree lit with colored bulbs.

But I am sure the chickadee that paused to watch me lasso and light the tree in the yard thought it was a strange business before he flew away from the top of the tree.

# GETTING IT RITE THE FIRST TIME

Hera, wife of Zeus, knew how to ring in the new year. By bathing annually in the spring of Canathus, she was able to reclaim her virginity. (It is an idea which cannot bear much thought.)

With the extreme case of Hera aside, ritual purification by water remains largely a symbolic act with which we are all in some way familiar.

It is ritual purification by fire with which we are probably less familiar. The ancients practiced a baptism by fire. The child was passed in and out of the flame in a symbolic conferring of immortality: All that was mortal was burned away; the spirit was freed from its prison of matter.

In *Walden*, Thoreau includes an account of a rite of purification by fire performed by the Mucclasse Indians of Georgia on the occasion of their new year.

The Mucclasse Indians celebrated their new year by taking all that was worn or broken and burning it. All left-over food was thrown into the fire and the village was swept clean. They then took laxatives and fasted for three days. When the fast was finished, all fires were extinguished. New fire was made and the new year began.

Thank Zeus and the ever-virgin Hera that such savage new year's rites have evolved into our more civilized Feast of the Falling Ball.

Nevertheless, I have never been fascinated by the falling ball. As I said goodnight to my hostess at a New Year's Eve party, the crowd in Times Square was chanting "5-4-3" on the TV behind me. Because I distracted her with parting praise for the texture of her dip and one last word about the Mucclasse Indians, she missed the televised ignition of the booster stage of the new year.

As I went out the door, I heard her weeping in her husband's arms that she was stuck in the old year and that he had gone into the new year without her. The woman apparently had the time-warp mentality of a Trekkie; it gave me the feeling that I was departing the Starship Enterprise instead of a brick rancher.

Through the closed door, I heard her scream that it was all the fault of the Mucclasse Indians.

I awoke on New Year's Day with the Mucclasse Indians still on my mind. I decided to search the house and gather together all the despicable things that were polluting my existence. Girt for battle in my bathrobe and armed with a cup of coffee and a brown bag to hold all that I planned to find, I set out across the vinyl tile wastes of the family room.

"What's Daddy doing?" the kids asked.

"He's having an idea," their mother said.

"Does this mean we have to hide in our rooms until the speeches are over like the last time?" they asked.

I was not deterred by their psychological flak.

Throughout the morning, the voices of little children could be heard crying: "I really need that rubber band" and "I like dolls without heads."

For many minutes my wife valiantly defended the junk drawer in the kitchen. When I finally broke through, I confiscated hundreds of little slotted and dated chips of plastic that had been used to seal the ends of bread bags.

"That does it!" my wife said. "If you want to throw things away, let's go to your den in the basement and have a look."

"No!" I moaned. But it was too late. She beat me down the steps and into the den. The clutter on my desk seemed to jump into her arms.

"I really need that old flashlight battery --sometimes it's a paperweight!" I said.

"Too late," she said. "Some Mucclasse Indian you would have made."

By lunch time a truce was declared. Everyone got his junk back. There was no purifying fire.

Perhaps I should be thankful for the advances of civilization which have freed us from all that is primitive and allow us to pass into a new year by merely watching a falling ball on television. Maybe if I give it a fair chance, I might discover, as countless Americans have, the true meaning of the falling ball.

Prompted by my new doubts about the merits of the Mucclasse way, I called my hostess of the night before to apologize.

"Don't worry," she said. "After you left, I saw the falling ball on instant-replay."

"Happy New Year," I said.

# KEEPING TRACK, JANUARY 1984

The ground is brick hard with cold and the tufts of grass are stiff, but the oldest boy is in the yard practicing casting with a Christmas fishing rod.

From the window, I can see the cranberry color of his hands. Soon he will come inside to warm his hands at the heat vent on the floor by the refrigerator, then he will go outside again.

Farther back in the yard, grackles are under the trees tossing up brown leaves with their beaks. Their sleek dark heads are iridescent like oil slicks.

So far this year there has been little activity at the bird feeder on a pole by the kitchen window. This is unusual. A 20-pound sack of wild bird food still sits unopened in the basement. The few birds that have come to the feeder are pecking yet at a few pounds of seed left over from last winter.

And the ears of decorative Indian corn, mottled red, purple, orange, white, removed from the house after Thanksgiving and placed on the back porch for the squirrels have hardly been touched.

Perhaps the device I recently made to keep squirrels from the feeder frightens the birds. For years, the squirrels would climb the pole to the feeder, shake out the seed and then feed on the ground.

They had learned quickly that a rap on the window or a threatening yell from the back porch was nothing to fear. Neighbors who had no idea of what was going on probably thought us a curious household oddly given several times a day to throwing open the back door and screaming into the wind.

To keep the squirrels from the bird feeder I mounted a barrier on the pole about a foot under it. The barrier is a thin wooden disc with a hole in the center, it hangs from the top of the pole on two thin wires. When a squirrel climbs the pole and reaches out and grabs the edge of the barrier, the disc tilts wildly to a steep squirrel-proof angle.

The thing actually works, but I think it is scaring the birds away. Now, of course, nothing is coming close to the feeder because of all the backyard fishing.

I am anxious, too, to use my Christmas gift, which is a used typewriter. I have had it with electric typewriters; we have two around the house that now do not work at all. I bought a reconditioned office-duty manual typewriter for less than the last two repair bills on the electrics.

My Christmas typewriter seems to be in good shape except for a dent in the carriage housing. I imagine that at sometime in its history a frustrated secretary gave it a whack with an axe.

I would like to be drafting this essay on it, but I am stuck by the window at the mission-control desk writing on a steno pad until my wife returns. The mission-control desk at our house is a stool at the kitchen counter.

It is easier to run a house with three small children from the kitchen counter than from anywhere else in the house. I pour juice, issue crackers, tie shoes, tell people what time it is.

It is good to have the clock back on the wall. During the holidays we took it down because it was the perfect spot for a large wreath made of pinecones and nuts. Out of habit we kept looking to the wreath for the time of day. We adapted poorly to Eastern Pinecone Time.

It is good once again to know what time it is, but I haven't the slightest idea why. It seems we have the urge in the face of the turmoil of life to look at a clock.

"It's hard to know what's going on in the world," the mind says, "but at least I know it's four o'clock."

Clock time is a universal understanding and there is in Chicago a clock maintained by the staff of the *Bulletin of the Atomic Scientists*.

It counts toward midnight the minutes remaining before an anticipated nuclear doomsday. It was advanced by one minute just this month to show an accelerating nuclear arms race and the breakdown in communications between Russia and America.

According to this clock, the Earth now has three metaphorical minutes left.

I have a friend who says we are destined to be progenitors of the universe. When the Earth blows, according to him, radiation will alter the already-peculiar genes now housed in our genetic-research laboratories. On the outward-bound debris of Earth will ride into space a phantasmagoria of radiant lifeforms and new worlds will be born.

This is preposterous, I think. But with three minutes left to go it is hard to know just what to think. There is orange juice spilled on the kitchen floor; the fishing line is in a tree and needs untangling, and it seems as we move into the future the odds are tilted against us at a somewhat squirrel-proof angle.

# A ONE-SKYROCKET HOLIDAY

There are certain things men must buy at certain times.

The faces of men who gather in drugstores before displays of chocolate-filled cardboard hearts show the dispassion associated with buying a bag of lawn fertilizer in the spring.

What's wrong with Valentine's Day, I think, is that it isn't very exciting. As presently observed, Valentine's Day is a one-skyrocket holiday, just a cut above Arbor Day.

Even the Roman church lost its enthusiasm for the day and scrapped observance of the feast of St. Valentine in 1969 during a housecleaning of the liturgical calendar.

The problem with St. Valentine was a case of identity. According to legend, there were two Valentines who lived in Italy in the third century. Both were martyred in 269 A.D. and had feasts celebrated on February 14.

One Valentine was a priest and physician of Rome and the other Valentine was the bishop of Terni. But it is speculated that they were actually a single saint divided by legends coming from two sources, the legend of the bishop of Terni being a later development of the life of the priest of Rome.

But this confusion and the insubstantial character of the legends cast a poor shadow under the megacandle light that burned after Vatican II, and St. Valentine was removed from the calendar of Catholic feasts.

Suspicions about Valentine existed long before. "What manner of person art thou?" cried Charles Lamb, the English essayist and critic in the salad days of the Nineteenth Century. "Art thou but a name, typifying the restless principle which impels poor humans to seek perfection in unions?"

Perfection in unions?

That comes as a heavy thought to this day when the holiday is all about going to the drugstore and buying two dollar's worth of chocolates packaged in six dollar's worth of cardboard.

"Mysterious personage!" roars Lamb in a Valentine ecstasy. "Like unto thee, assuredly, there is no other mitred father in the calendar."

Lamb knew there was something vague about Valentine long before Vatican II, but he thought the mystery a marvelous delight.

Did the demise of the feast of St. Valentine affect Valentine's Day?

Of course not. Other than lending a name, St. Valentine has little to do with Valentine's Day.

The day had its origin more than likely in a Christianizing of the pagan Lupercalia, a festival of ancient Rome celebrated on February 15.

Lupercus was not a Roman god and that negative fact is about all we know of him. It is believed that even to the Romans he was a misty figure, as legendary to them as St. Valentine is to us. Lupercalia was a celebration of fertility which possibly evolved from an older rite designed to keep wolves away from the city, since Luperci, the name of the priests, can be translated as wolf-averter and part of the Lupercalian ritual seems to have little to do with fertility.

The curious rite of Lupercus began with the sacrifice of several goats and a single dog by the Luperci. Two priests had their foreheads dabbed with blood from the knives. The blood was then washed away with wool soaked in milk. Then they were required to laugh. Later, thongs were cut from the skins of the sacrificed animals. The Luperci then took off their clothes and ran around the walls of the old Palatine city striking people with the thongs. It was believed that a woman struck by the thongs would be cured of sterility.

During the day there was orgiastic feasting. The popular food of the holiday was pork-and-pine nut sausage flavored with cumin and pepper. The sausage was so strongly associated with Lupercalia that when Constantine the Great embraced Christianity early in the Fourth Century, he bent to the will of the church fathers who were trying to stamp out pagan practices and he prohibited the eating of sausages in Rome. (St. Patrick would later imitate, I suppose, Constantine's driving the sausages out of Rome by driving the snakes out of Ireland.)

Lupercalia was finally outlawed in 494 A.D. and Pope Gelasius I replaced it with the feast of the Purification. This feast was later moved back to February 2 and it was probably not long after that when the feast of St. Valentine emerged as a substitute holiday for Lupercalia. The association of St. Valentine with love possibly came from the fertility element of the old festival.

In later centuries there was a pleasant belief that it was on St. Valentine's Day that the birds chose their mates. Verses from Chaucer, Shakespeare and others attest to this old belief.

I think that what we need to do to enliven our present Valentine's Day is draw a little from each of the old traditions.

Perhaps we could celebrate by buying two canaries, feasting on sausage and running around the block naked. The more muddled the holiday, the merrier, I think.

And the heck with chocolate candy.

# WHY GREEN BEER

Saint Patrick's Day is celebrated religiously in churches and viciously in pubs. The patron saint of Ireland and the pagan Bacchus, the god of wine, have been married in our minds into a sort of Jolly Green Giant who is the patron saint of saloons.

I got my drop of green blood from my mother's father, whose parents were Irish immigrants. After a day in the Pennsylvania coal mines, he celebrated St. Patrick's Day moderately by listening to the Irish music and Pat-and-Mike jokes broadcast late at night by radio from the Hotel Casey in Scranton.

Green beer (because of the color) is not my favorite drink, but I do force myself to swallow a glass or two of it. St. Patrick would not be properly honored if I did anything less.

It was George Carlin who mused on one of his comedy records about why there isn't any blue food. I think about Carlin's monologue every St. Patrick's Day as I rip apart my wife's cabinets looking for the little box of food colorings.

I always prepare a pitcher of green beer before supper on St. Patrick's Day. Because I have messed up the kitchen looking for the food coloring and the little pitcher, a bit of commotion always surrounds my annual making of green beer. And the kids ask a lot of unanswerable questions about why I don't make orange beer on Halloween and red beer on Valentine's Day.

For years, I always made green beer with green food coloring. I always wondered, as I stood in the kitchen drinking my token glass of neon-green beer, why my green beer didn't look quite the same as the green beer you get in a bar.

It was just two years ago I finally learned that you don't make green beer with green food coloring. You make green beer with *blue* coloring.

When you mix the blue of the coloring with the yellow of the beer, you get green. If you mix green food coloring with beer, you get chartreuse. For years, I had celebrated the saint's day in ignorant bliss with chartreuse beer.

For supper on St. Patrick's Day, we always have corned beef and cabbage. I like corned beef and cabbage even less than I like green beer, so we only have it once a year on St. Patrick's Day.

The kids once asked why --if I didn't like either green beer or corned beef and cabbage-- I went through with St. Patrick's Day. I told them it was the price you paid for being a Christian.

But my wife found a way of making corned beef and cabbage into a delicacy for me not long ago. She came up with a creamy horseradish sauce that we ladle into the folds of the large steaming wedges of cabbage and pour over the corned beef.

Our collection of Irish music, which we play as a backdrop to the beef, cabbage and beer, consists of two quite different record albums.

The Bing Crosby record contains songs that reflect the sunny side of the Irish mystique, like "MacNamara's Band" and "When Irish Eyes Are Smiling." Although the album is a recent release, the recordings are very old, the fidelity poor by today's standards. It sounds a lot like the old time radio music my grandfather heard coming live from the Hotel Casey. That's why I like it.

Our other album mirrors the dark side of Irish life. It is a recording of a Carnegie Hall concert given in 1962 by The Clancey Brothers and Tommy Makem. It's real Irish folk music, closer to the bone of Ireland than "It's the Same Old Shillelagh" as sung by Bing Crosby.

One song on the album, "The Patriot Game," written by poet Dominic Behan, brother of playwright Brendan, begins:

*Come all you young rebels and list' while I sing,*

*For the love of one's country is a terrible thing.*

*It banishes fear with the speed of a flame,*

*And it makes us all part of the patriot game.*

It is the bitter, dying thought of a teen-aged rebel lying on the ground with his body full of holes. He feels betrayed by the heroic glamour which lured him into the service of the I.R.A. and quickly brought his youth to a trivial end.

Although much of the music has images of violence and death, there are a few cheery, rollicking songs about whiskey and girls.

On St. Patrick's Day, I would prefer not to think of the horror that is Ireland. I will, instead, attend to the making of green beer and the eternal Irish mystery of "Who Threw the Overalls in Mrs. Murphy's Chowder?" That song is on the Crosby record.

# ON BALANCE, HAPPINESS

A few years ago when the youngest child was a toddler in diapers, he received a greeting card with a mug of beer and a golf club on it.

And judging from subsequent cards, I think the sender has the same riverboat approach to selecting greeting cards as I do: Pick a card --any card-- and be done with it.

But I recently received what seemed to me a thoughtfully selected greeting card that featured a line from Nathaniel Hawthorne: "Happiness is a butterfly which when pursued is just beyond your grasp...but if you sit down quietly, may alight upon you." I find Hawthorne's appearance on a birthday card remarkable since most of what he wrote would be appropriate for celebrating First Sin or the birth of an illegitimate child.

Even though I am not sure what Hawthorne means, the line contains an intriguing metaphor which creates an aura of wisdom. Many writers, I think, add lines like this to their works with the hope of appearing on greeting cards. Here's an example: Truth is a river with a muddy bottom.

I made that up in three seconds. I don't know what it means but it sounds good. Here is a variation: Truth is river that has no bottom. I don't know what that means either.

Nevertheless, these seem to be two very wise sayings about truth. And I imagine that if I took a minute to write a dozen more wise sayings, some sort of cult would spring up around me.

The trick to wise sayings is to include a metaphor, a comparison between two seemingly dissimilar things --such as hope and a butterfly, truth and a river. Anyone can do it. Poets, for instance, use many metaphors, which gives them the appearance of wisdom when they are probably no wiser than anyone else. If poets were indeed wise, we would certainly have a third house of government, the Poets:

"During a press conference this morning, Senator Fuelrod denounced the stand of the House of Poets on nuclear proliferation. But Poet majority whip Sam Trochee later replied, 'Peace is a river with a muddy bottom.' This reflects a significant change in the thinking of the House of Poets which for so long maintained that peace was a river that had no bottom. What exactly is on the bottom of the river of peace? Does it even have a bottom? This issue will be examined tonight at 11:30 by Ted Koppel in a special report, 'The River of Peace: What Are They Talking About?' "

This, I guess, is why there is no House of Poets.

But what Hawthorne said about happiness is worth consideration. The only problem with the line, though, is the butterfly. Butterflies are sissy things for men to write about. He should have used something more macho, like a horse: "Happiness is a horse which when pursued is just beyond your grasp...but if you sit down quietly, may alight upon you."

That would have been far better.

But pursuing happiness in any form is very American. America was founded on a belief in the primacy of "life, liberty and the pursuit of happiness." Though Hawthorne seems subversive in suggesting that happiness not be actively pursued, Nat Hawthorne was by all reports a good American. Had he lived earlier and helped Tom Jefferson draft the Declaration of Independence, I am sure the document would have informed George III of our belief in "life, liberty and the right to quietly await the butterfly of happiness."

George probably would have sent the Whitecoats instead of the Redcoats.

But waiting around for happiness to alight is not the American way. Pursuing happiness is the American way. And we have gotten much better at it since Hawthorne's day.

I like to stop at the 7-Eleven store out on the highway on summer nights. It's a great place to observe America passing. The store is air-conditioned and the lights are fluorescently cool against the hot, heavy-smelling country air. The parking lot is filled with cars with hot engines and rich automotive smells. The people keep coming and going. Some buy beer and what my kids call ferris-wheel hot dogs from the counter rotisserie. Then they move on in the night. Some men are bare chested. Some women wear bathing suits. The windshields of their cars are spattered with road moths and, I guess, the butterflies of happiness.

France so kindly sent us the Statue of Liberty. Perhaps some country will send us a Statue of Happiness. Perhaps it will be a sphinx-like amalgam of a horse and butterfly. With a rider holding aloft a mug of beer and a golf club.

# DISTANT BEACONS

# BATHTUB MELONS, DANCING CRABS

Furlongs and fathoms won't do. Hands are for horses and cubits are for arks. But how big is a watermelon? Pounds just don't say enough.

The supermarkets advertise whole watermelons. If you buy by the slice, quarter or half, you buy by the pound. But if you buy by the watermelon, you buy by the *whole*. In these .05-per-cent and to-the-millimeter times, the *whole* is a welcome measure.

It is the duty of a good Baltimore father to teach his children about buying watermelons, especially when the purchase is made by the whole. My father, in those days when a watermelon was as big as a bathtub, was a very fussy buyer.

He took me to the piers on Pratt Street where the melons came in small open boats across the Chesapeake Bay from the Eastern Shore to Baltimore. He made the barechested man on the boat plug the watermelon before he bought it. The man would step with a rocking gait among the piles of watermelon on the boat sitting low in the water. The man would come to a bright green melon. He would slip his knife into the melon four times at an angle. Then he would stab the plug with his knife and present it to my father. He would throw the watermelon onto the pier as my father examined the plug, a wet red pyramid on a long knife. My father would stoop and thump the melon with his finger before he nodded and the man replaced the plug in the watermelon.

Thus was I taught to buy a watermelon by the *whole*.

The other duty of a good Baltimore father is to teach his children about buying crabs. The crabs of past-remembered were as big as a baseball glove. Their claws were blue and white. Whenever my father was given a live hard crab that couldn't tap dance, he would argue with the man that it was dead.

"This crab is dead," he said.

"All my crab's alive. You gotta take him."

My father put the crab on the floor of the crab store that was just a few blocks up from the waterfront.

"If that crab can't dance, I'm not taking him."

I remember feeling a little scared at the time. The man was not happy. My father took the crab from the counter and sat him on the floor.

"He's dead," my father said.

"That crab's alive," the man said.

"Then you come out here and make him walk," my father said. "You make this crab walk or I'm not taking him."

I am beginning to wonder what I really learned about crabs and watermelons. I find myself taking pre-steamed crabs in paper bags without even counting them. And just the other day I took the kids to the supermarket to buy a watermelon. I moved the spare tire in the trunk before I left so I could bring it home. I ended up carrying it out of the store in a brown bag in one hand.

A dozen steamed crabs is smaller, too. Now a dozen crabs seems a pathetic little pile in the middle of the table. The price is not pathetic. The night I dumped a much ballyhooed dozen crabs on the table, the price I paid matched what my father and mother were each making in wages for a seven-day week at a Baltimore defense plant during the war.

My father married a girl from Scranton during the war. Up in Scranton they didn't know that newspaper was the proper table covering for eating crabs and watermelon. Actually, up in Scranton they didn't know what to do with crabs. They had never seen a Baltimore steamed crab. They also ate watermelon on plates with forks.

My father used to bring watermelons as big as bathtubs to Scranton when we would visit my grandparents. He would take over the kitchen table after supper and throw my grandfather's funny-looking Scranton newspaper that had different comics than the Baltimore *Sun* over the table.

"This is the way they do it in Baltimore," my mother would say indulgently.

# THE HOUND OF THE POHLNERVILLES

It was not by chance that my simple life flashed before me at a tire center on Belair Road.

My father is fond of saying he got a handshake for his birthday and two for Christmas when he was a kid. But I believe there is some exaggeration in the stories I get from my father about how bad things used to be. He is the kind of guy who walked through a lot of snow to get to school.

My paternal grandparents had 10 children and they all lived in a row house on Robinson Street in Highlandtown. There, according to my father's version of how it used to be, a wolf stood on the scrubbed marble steps with cleanser dust on its paws, its steaming muzzle fogging the glass in the front door.

It's my father's eight sisters who seem best at setting the record straight. Although my eight aunts went to the same school as my father, the snow they had to walk through to get there in their stories is never as deep as the snow my father had to walk through. They say he must have walked on the other side of the street. And none of them remembers having to chase a wolf away when it was time to scrub the steps.

From the stories of the eight sisters, I have come to believe that thinking poor, as opposed to actually being poor, more accurately describes my inherited self-image. It would be better to say that Grandfather Pohlner, a German immigrant working as a pattern cutter in a Baltimore sweatshop, didn't have much money and that Nanny Pohlner sewed long into the night making dresses for eight girls to make ends meet.

As a consequence of living among wolves in a land of deep snow, my father became a two-job-when-necessary, no-frills-and-nonsense man. Once when I was in college, I told him that I had seen a briar pipe at Fader's that cost a hundred dollars. I told him that I hoped when I got out of college, I would be able to afford a pipe like that.

"If you ever spend a hundred dollars on a pipe, no matter how rich you get, I'll beat knots on your head," he said.

He got his point across. To this day, I smoke only inexpensive Dr. Grabows pulled from a clip-card at the drugstore.

It was all this that went through my mind in the tire center when the man said, "Do you want to go the extra money for whitewalls or not?"

I wanted to say, "Well in my family, we don't spend money on nonsense." The line came to mind with motto-like quickness.

But, according to a recent letter from my life insurance company, I am halfway through my life. Their actuaries are on the ball. And their computer writes a nice letter, too. As I stood there, inhaling rubber fumes with half of my life gone down the drain, I realized that I had never owned whitewall tires.

"Are they any better than black tires?" I asked in what sounded strangely like my father's voice.

"Why sure they are," the tire man said. "Just like colored stripes on over-priced sneakers, whitewalls make you go faster, look younger, and make it a cinch to pick up chicks."

I thought he might be kidding, but he had a real funeral-director look on his face. I bought the whitewalls.

As I pulled away, I saw the reflection of the family sedan in the large window of the tire center. The car *did* look good. And as I touched the accelerator, I could tell that both the car and I had been imbued with youth. That tire man knew more about life than I had imagined. I chided myself for having wasted time on Aquinas, Sartre and Donahue. That tire man had some answers.

At home, I noticed as I stood back from the parked car how the whitewalls made the car appear to be in motion even when it was standing still in the driveway. Even the children's car seat strapped in the back and a petrified, half-dissolved green lollipop with a broken stick that was stuck on the rear window could not detract from the raciness that the new whitewalls gave the car.

Now all I had to do was try my hand at picking up chicks.

I chased a large stray dog with short, pointed ears off the front porch as I went into the house. It had a strange white powder on its paws.

"Hey baby," I cried with a leer in my voice.

"Would you rinse out the diapers for me?" she whispered gently from upstairs so as not to wake up the baby.

I stood at the laundry tub in the basement. Some largeness, some puffiness inside of me, began to shrink and wrinkle upon itself like a dying balloon.

Maybe, just maybe I thought, the snow my father walked through really was that deep.

# CATCHER IN THE WHEAT

Once upon a time in a TV commercial, like Mother Nature in tight jeans, Sandy Duncan strolled in a field of bright wheat holding a wand of wheat in her hand and reflecting aloud about crackers and her life.

The heart of this TV commercial was the innocent wonder Sandy Duncan expressed about how she has grown up and is now doing a commercial for the very same brand of wheat crackers her parents kept around the house when she was a kid.

There is no deep meaning in it. Wonder simply exists --like a balloon on a string. You couldn't watch this commercial without reminiscing about the crackers of your own youth.

I guess my parents didn't like the kind of wheat cracker Sandy Duncan's parents favored. I mostly remember saltines.

It was always my impression as a child that the fellow who invented saltines also invented canned noodle soup because they were always served together and both were difficult to eat.

Saltines-and-noodle soup was a frustrating combination because in very little hands a saltine would always split and shatter all over the table and floor before you got much of it into your mouth. And two-inch-long noodles are impossible for a child to catch with a spoon. Actually, two-inch noodles are impossible for anyone to catch with anything.

Most people I know had this experience and they all seem to remember a mother's voice saying, "Why aren't you eating your lunch?" To which they all recall replying, "I'm trying! I'm trying!" as noodles well-slicked in chicken broth slipped back into the bowl and the cracker dust flew. No matter how many times my mother stormed over to my bowl with a butter knife to cut my soup, it still didn't work.

It was the kind of thing you were moved to remember as Sandy Duncan described every facet of her wheat crackers against a background of Elysian music. It was not the only thing I was moved to remember.

The three most well-known Grahams, I imagine, are Billy, Martha and Sheila. Few know of the great American, Sylvester Graham (1794-1851), who was the father of the graham cracker, sort of.

Sylvester Graham was regarded as a bit of a crackpot in his day as he traveled the East Coast lecturing on temperance, cholera, anatomy and the virtues of hard mattresses and clean living.

He also was a dietary pioneer. Unlike his lectures on temperance and clean living, his torchlight speeches extolling the wonders of flour made from the *whole* kernel of wheat, which everyone came to call graham flour, after him, created such a stir that graham bread became a hot item.

Although Sylvester Graham's birthday was never honored at my kindergarten (because it occurs in July when school is out), the ritualistic eating of graham crackers was a part of the curriculum.

Graham crackers were dispensed daily along with fat little bottles of milk with cardboard-disc stoppers. Opening the milk bottles was as much fun as eating noodle soup and saltines.

The wheat cracker Sandy Duncan sold on TV is not the same kind of wheat cracker as the graham cracker which is traditionally eaten in kindergarten.

Even though she associated her wheat cracker with the innocence of her youth, she couldn't go all the way and mention kindergarten, the ultimate innocent cracker experience, as that little bit of Holden Caulfield in all of us expected her to do as she patrolled the amber waves of grain like a catcher in the wheat.

I think that no one in my kindergarten ever consciously ate the graham crackers. We ate them absently as we bit them into shapes. It was the thing to do.

We boys mostly bit our crackers until they looked like pistols. Then we shot each other. After that, we took our required naps by laying our heads in the crumbs and milk dots on the table. We did this every day.

I guess that wouldn't make a good Sandy-Duncan-type cracker commercial.

Inspired by the Sandy Duncan commercial, I once tried to sell my memories of saltines and grahams to a few cracker companies. As a writer, I can withstand the blow of a rejected manuscript, but to receive letters rejecting my youth is another thing. I bow to Sandy Duncan, her crackers and her youth, deeply.

# RAGS, BOTTLES AND BONES

Youth is as dark as it is bright.

To Scranton, where my grandparents lived among miners and railroad men, I made long visits when I was small. My grandparents rented the upper right quarter of a large house that was owned by a magician who lived downstairs with his wife. His warehouse full of carnival supplies was at the end of the yard by the shed that held barrels of ashes. A muddy alley lay to the left. To the right, behind a wire fence, was a truckyard, paved with cinders. At night, as I sat in my grandparents' bathtub, the day's trash from the four apartments was burned in a barrel in the yard below. As I sat in the tub, I could part the curtains in a little window and see the fire and the shadow of the magician.

At night, from the room off the kitchen where I slept, I watched the coal burn in the stove with a gassy blue flame behind the tooth-like vents. Once, before the door was pushed open for the night, talk filtered through the door about the aunt of someone in the family. She had lived not far away. While her husband was at work, three men came to her house in a car. Without saying goodbye to her children, she left in the car and was never seen or heard from again.

Some days, the devil's wagon, as it was called, came down the alley. The driver was known to lash out with his whip at children. I was to watch from the porch upstairs, warned to peep over the railing and not let him see me. There were stories of Indians still living in the mountains. One had kidnaped a child. Whether or not the driver was an Indian, I do not know. But the story of the Indians was whispered once when the driver appeared in the alley with his highsided wagon. He would wind a long trumpet and crack his whip in the air to announce himself. Between horn blasts of a long, single note, he would call out something I couldn't understand. I was told he was saying, "Rags, bottles and bones."

In Baltimore, where my parents lived by Clifton Park, the alley between the rows of houses often had gypsies who danced carefully around the horse manure. At the first sound of a tambourine, I was always called into the house and had to watch from the window. The children were also made to stay away from the knife and scissor sharpener who carried his stone on a wooden frame on his back.

The tailor's shop at the end of the alley constantly poured steam from a vent in the back yard. Other openings issued hissing noises and sudden bursts of steam. There was talk up and down the front porches one night about something that had happened in the tailor's shop. What had happened was never mentioned. The children were told never to talk to the tailor or go into his shop. I was surprised at a later time when I was told to take my father's suit there to be cleaned, but I was warned to leave the store as soon as I gave the suit to the tailor.

In Baltimore County, where I was mostly raised, the countryside beyond my parents' new brick rowhouse was being chewed at by building machines. In the country around us were ruined houses and small graveyards that seemed to sit in the middle of nowhere. In the old houses, my friends and I played. We fought our way through brambles and weeds higher than ourselves to get near. Front and back steps had rotted away from most of the old houses. It took planning and effort to climb into them.

We looked at yellowed newspapers and magazines we found in the attics. We examined every room in every house. We sifted through rubbish, knew everything and pieced together the story of each house. We knew the house with the rusty knife. We knew the house where the milky-looking mirror had been left hanging on the wall.

I never had a sense of time or place when I explored the ruined houses that seemed to sit inexplicably in desolation. I was never able to grasp how, just by turning down the right path or two within a mile of my parents' house, I could suddenly be in a broad and alien land my parents would never understand, in places where my father's car couldn't go, that couldn't be seen from the car window no matter what road we drove on a Sunday afternoon.

Darkness and mystery are no longer a part of my clockwork and fluorescent life. It is something I am too old to ever touch again. Even the reaching hand of memory comes back almost empty --with hardly a smudge on a finger to prove that all the darkness was true.

# PENATES AND CRACKERJACKS

The penates were household guardians, the kitchen gods of the ancient Romans. A shrine with images of the penates could be found in the kitchens of most homes in old Rome.

The Roman penates belong to yesterday, of course, but the idea of having kitchen gods has, I think, survived.

My father's kitchen god is Chuck Thompson. He speaks to my father from a radio atop the refrigerator. Chuck Thompson, the voice of the Baltimore Orioles, has been up on the refrigerator talking to my father for as long as I can remember.

Though refrigerators came and went when I was kid, Chuck was always there. Over the objections of my mother, who did not like baseball, he would speak from his perch during Sunday dinners, visits from old aunts who were hard of hearing, the singing of Happy Birthday.

"Turn that man off," my mother would say.

"I'll just turn him down a little," my father would say.

Although I played Little League ball and collected baseball cards when I was a kid, I was never really an Orioles fan. I was never so glad as that day many years ago when I finally left my father's house and knew that I would never again have to live with the omnipresent voice of Chuck Thompson.

My father has always been a little disappointed that I am not a baseball fan. He worries now that my little children will catch my shameful uninterest in baseball. When he comes to visit, he often checks up on me by playing a little ball with the kids in the yard to see how sharp they are.

On a Saturday morning, if I say to the kids, "Let's play baseball after breakfast," they know what's happening. "Grandpa must be coming to visit tomorrow!" they say. As my wife prepares for my mother with wax and Windex, I make ready for my father in my own way.

Although I am not what people call "sports minded," I do like to play baseball with the kids. This year they are finally old enough to play with hard balls, wooden bats and leather gloves. No more plastic bats and big rubber balls.

Now that we are playing real hardball --as my aluminum siding will attest-- and you don't get one more chance after you strike out, I find myself sounding like Mr. Baseball as I give tips about positioning feet, holding bats and other baseball business:

"Look before you throw the ball!"

"No crying!  Rub it off!"

"When you're out, you're out!"

Because of all the green interest in baseball around the house this year, I took the kids to Memorial Stadium a few weeks ago to see their first big-league baseball game.  They wanted to see the Orioles.  I hadn't been to the stadium in almost 20 years and I was looking forward just a little to seeing a game myself.  A ball game every 20 years or so I can take.

At the stadium I pointed out the broadcast booth between decks to the kids.  I told them to look for a man with a hat.  As everyone in Baltimore knows, Chuck Thompson doesn't even take a shower without a hat.  It's his trademark.  After a while, we convinced ourselves that we had seen Chuck Thompson.

"That's the man who talks to Grandpa on the radio," I told them.  I turned on a little transistor radio which was very hard to hear amid the noise and let the kids take turns holding it to their ears to listen to Chuck as I pointed to the broadcast booth and tried to explain radio waves.

Chuck still talks to my father.  The other day when I visited my parents, he was out in the kitchen talking to my father from the top of the refrigerator.  If it weren't for Chuck, I guess the house would be pretty quiet now that all the children have gone.

"Turn that man off so people can talk," my mother said when I came in.

"I'll just turn him down a little," my father said.

# THOSE QUIET, DIM SUMMER EVENINGS

A summer evening, I think, was once a more formal time.

After supper, we children were given baths and dressed in clean clothes. We were warned to play in a restrained manner and to keep our clothes clean. There was to be no yelling, running around, playing in the dirt. We were expected to ride our bicycles up and down the front sidewalk under the thick leaves of the trees that lined both sides of the street.

Before I was seven years old, the gas street lamps were replaced with electric lights. The new electric light by our house was too bright for the man who lived next door. He fastened a bucket to a pole and, like an altar boy, religiously snuffed the new electric candle every night.

My mother always worried that the man would get into trouble for putting the bucket over the light and that we would get into trouble because the light was by our house.

The street lights came on when it was almost dark. For a while, when the electric lights were new, keeping track of the exact time they came on was a neighborhood preoccupation. When the lights came on, the men would look at their watches and say what time it was. I asked who turned the street lights on and was told about wires that went all the way into the city. It was a large idea.

The milky globes on the electric street lights did not have to be washed, whereas the clear glass shield on the old gas lamps had to be cleaned on a regular basis. Watching the man wash the fragile looking glass bowls of the gas lights was something we did during our summers. The man walked the streets with a ladder, pail and rag. He brought the globe down from the top of the light, washed it on the ground, then took it back up the ladder.

There were four men who were watched closely during the summer by the little children in my old neighborhood. We watched the man who washed the street lights, the fat man who bounced kegs of beer off a truck onto a thick rubber pad and rolled them into the basement window of the corner saloon, the man who tarred roofs and gave us chips of tar to chew, and the iceman.

The iceman never gave us chips of ice. We waited until he had gone up the back path to a house with a block of ice between tongs slung over his shoulder. Then we climbed up the back of the truck and filled our hands with little pieces of ice. Some of the ice we put in our mouths. We rubbed the rest of it on our sunburned arms. Such were our days.

Then the lights were turned off in the houses in the evening after the children were bathed and dressed in crisp clothes. People sat on their front porches. It was quiet. The man next door would come out and put the pail-and-pole contraption over the street light and it would be dark by our house. We would ride our bikes up the street to Harford Road and watch little brightly colored men in the distance playing softball in Clifton Park.

When it was darker, when we had lingered too long at the corner and knew that everyone would be wondering where we had gone, we watched the streetcars across the street come and go on the tracks along the edge of the park. They were rectangles of framed light. We listened to the sound the brakes made when they were dropped onto the tracks.

Of course, there were lightning bugs and ice cream trucks. There were pictures inside the lids of the Dixie cups. I never recognized any of the people, but I always licked the lids and studied the pictures anyway.

Once the *New York Times* ran an editorial called "Magic Hours." The *Times* suggested that Daylight Saving Time be increased by an additional hour during the summer months to save fuel and "swell the magic of summer." Both time and money would be saved.

But I don't like the idea. Little kids would have to go to bed long before dark with that system. For them, the magic of a summer evening would not be swelled; it would be eliminated. One of the magical aspects of a summer evening is the gathering of darkness and forming of stillness.

Although people don't sit on front porches the way they used to, and kids are not bathed and dressed for the evenings that no longer seem to be honored with Sunday reverence, to remove nightfall from summer evenings, even in the name of economy, is unacceptable.

There are still those who save fuel by turning out the lights and sitting outside. They also know that watching night form with clean hands and a clean shirt is not a waste of time.

# TEA MYTHS

The Japanese tea myth is a somewhat grisly story.

Bodhidharma, a Chinese Buddhist saint, was so enraged with himself for falling asleep during a period of meditation that he severed his eyelids so that such a thing would never happen again. When the shells of skin fell to the ground, they rooted and grew into the first tea plants.

Although tea, a real eye-opening drink, has come to be a bit like peas porridge in that some like it hot and some like it cold, I am sure that Bodhidharma never envisioned cold cans of tea laced with a rust-inhibiting chemical dropping with a rush of dull plinks and clacks from a soda machine.

Using the orange-juice-isn't-just-for-breakfast-anymore advertising ploy, Dandy Don Meredith square danced into a glow all one winter on TV to convince us that iced tea isn't just for summer anymore. (Surely, we will be told some day that radial tires aren't just for cars anymore.)

Because tradition is a heavy stone in the tray of any balance, I can't help wondering if many people had the courage to drink iced tea last winter. But all that is behind us. In the middle of the summer, there is no question about the propriety of drinking iced tea.

What is so peculiar about iced tea is that no two people seem to be able to produce a glass of the stuff that tastes the same. Despite the simplicity of its composition, iced tea, like the two-ingredient martini, is a very quirky drink.

Most of us had our tastes for iced tea formed by mom's stovetop brew. Anything you come across that doesn't taste just like mom's isn't...well, it just isn't iced tea. It's something you drink to be polite when you are a guest.

"How do these people drink this?" you think to yourself when you are visiting.

With what I realize now to have been a considerable expenditure of fossil fuel, my mother used to boil water in a very large pot for what seemed to be an entire afternoon to make iced tea. Many dinosaurs lived and died beyond the border of comprehension to make a few mahogany-colored gallons of her tea.

My mother's pot with its simple contents of water and tea bags --whose number grew as the afternoon wore on-- seemed to require as much attention and tasting as if it were a pot of split-pea soup or spaghetti sauce. She began with a pot of water and a dozen tea bags whose strings were knotted together. The bags were dropped into the water and the mass of little tags on the other ends of the strings hung outside over the edge of the pot. She would turn on the stove and then, as it always seemed to me, go down into the basement to iron clothes.

Later, on her way upstairs with the first armload of pressed clothes on hangers, she would stop by the pot and taste the tea with a soup spoon. "Dishwater," she would say. She would add more tea bags to the pot. On her way back down to the basement, she would taste it again. She would shiver like a man downing a double toot of bourbon and add a few glasses of water.

This would go on all afternoon.

When my sister was married, she received a solar-powered iced tea maker as a gift. The device is simpler than it sounds. You can sort of duplicate the thing by putting a tea bag in a canning jar full of water, screwing the lid down tightly and setting it on the back porch in the sun in the morning. When you come home from work, you pour the contents of the jar into a glass filled with ice cubes and you have iced tea.

My mother beheld the gift somewhat skeptically. I am willing to bet that in her will she has bequeathed her tall and dented iced tea pot to my sister.

My wife makes iced tea in a manner which seems to strike a compromise between my mother's ferocious hot-water assault on the tea of China and my sister's namby-pamby solar-powered maker. She soaks a few tea bags in a small carafe of hot water to make a concentrate that is diluted in the glass when it is served.

We don't measure when we pour the concentrate. And we don't like lemon or sugar in our iced tea. We don't even like mint, though we grow it by the side door for guests and because our parents always grew mint.

I know from all the fiddling around with sugar spoons, lemon wedges and trips to the kitchen tap that more than one visitor has thought what they would never say: How do these people drink this?

A little kid at a cookout last year in our yard spit her first mouthful of our iced tea onto our lawn.

I wondered if myths worked backwards when she did it. I wondered if from the little sodden spot in the grass there might rise a Buddhist saint. Or Don Meredith.

Nothing happened, but the message was clear.

# SHEAR HORROR

My last haircut was on the Day of the Ice-Skating Goose.

Because I don't like haircuts and get them as infrequently as possible, they are marked and remembered by events of domestic significance.

Early on the morning of the last haircut, a flight of north-bound geese flew over the house. One of the geese was struggling to join the flying V and it looked like a skater in an ice show who had stumbled and was trying to get back into a speeding formation. In my mind, I applauded the goose as it regained the flight pattern and took its place between the fourth and fifth goose on the east side of the V.

But ice skaters and geese got all mixed up in the telling of the story to the children later at breakfast and that Saturday became known as the Day of the Ice-Skating Goose. My previous haircut was on the Day the Antifreeze Spilled on the Driveway. Every haircut has a story.

My aversion to haircuts may well lie in the past. It was during the 1950s when the price of a haircut climbed to 60 cents that my father brought into the house a box of tools that ruined my appearance and my life for many years. He had gone to Sears Roebuck and bought a barber kit.

No longer would I walk with the neighborhood gang on Saturday mornings to the barber shop. I would miss the comic books. There were stacks of comic books at the barber shop. But the barbers wouldn't let you in to read them unless you were getting a haircut.

My father cut hair in the basement under a bare 100-watt lightbulb. There were no comic books, no neighborhood kids with baseball caps sitting around. There were no strangely shaped bottles of hair tonics or display cards with colored combs with silver clips to look at. I would look instead at the white wisps of cobwebs in the rafters and wonder why you never saw the spiders.

His barber chair was an old loose-jointed stool that swayed precariously and it was mounted on a box. It was a rickety affair that did not meet my mother's approval. Actually, the whole do-it-yourself barber business did not meet her approval because I never returned from the basement looking at all as she remembered me. Here and there would be a white line of exposed scalp.

But once you were lifted onto the box-and-stool rig, your fate was sealed. There was no way you could get down without killing yourself. Whenever my wailing and my father's threats to knock my block off (the ultimate haircut) got really bad, my mother would come to my defense and call above the din, "Pay the money! Pay the money!" from the top of the basement stairs.

But my father did not believe in paying anyone to do anything he could do himself. He would cut hair with a buzzing clipper in one hand and a sheet of instructions that had little pictures of a guy getting a haircut in the other.

I was returned to the ranks of my friends by the time I was in high school, but most of them were no longer going to the old barber shop just up the street. Adolescents are self-conscious about their appearance and the old ("I know what your mother wants") barbers would not take instructions from the neighborhood kids.

But there was a barber shop at some distance where they would listen to you. Adolescents are always looking for someone to listen to them and are willing to walk a mile for a little respect. If you told the barbers at the new place that you wanted to look like Ricky Nelson or one of the Everly Brothers, they knew what you meant and they did their best. At the end they would rub your head with an odoriferous hair tonic that today reminds me of a mixture of red-light perfume and sewing machine oil. Then they would slick it all back with a long comb, spin the chair around to face the mirror and it was Hello, Mary Lou.

I stopped going to barber shops when the Beatles popularized a hair style that hadn't been the rage since the Middle Ages. For almost 10 years I cut my own hair because with that style no one could tell if you had made a mistake or not.

Eventually I returned to the barber shop. But I don't like it. I am one of those people who has to take a shower immediately after a hair cut. It doesn't bother some people, but I can't stand spending a day with hair snippets under my collar and with little piles of hair inside my ears. And there is still this fear that if I move around in the chair too much, the barber might knock my block off.

"Do you want to look like a rock star or somethin'?" the barber asked.

You've got to go with the flow, I guess, but I just asked for a regular haircut. I don't think there is any musical movement associated with a "regular" haircut. I listened to the buzz of the clipper. There was no song to sing on the Day of the Ice-Skating Goose.

# STEPPING AHEAD

Kids today take lessons in everything from aerobics to oat rolling and you get the idea that their future is going to be a cheery place with everyone twirling batons and doing back-flips as they go about their business. Life in the future should resemble the old Ed Sullivan Show.

I don't recall there being much in the way of "lessons" when I was a kid. Piano lessons don't count because they were not taken seriously.

Some kids in my old neighborhood took piano lessons, but none of them ever learned too much, as best as I can remember. I don't think their parents really expected them to learn to play the piano. Making kids take piano lessons is a traditional thing and the custom is so ancient it may even predate the invention of the piano itself.

I only had one lesson when I was a kid. It wasn't a piano lesson. It was a tap dance lesson that cost a quarter.

A man who seemed to have slipped off Broadway from "The Music Man," sounding like Robert Preston in the role of Professor Harold Hill probably (my memory of all this is dim), came to my grammar school with the grand scheme of teaching the whole school to tap dance.

The thought of a whole parochial school that could tap dance apparently appealed to the nuns. I don't know why. (This was decades before the innovations of Vatican II).

What the Dancing Man said to the sisters that gave them the notion that the whole school could tap dance or even needed to tap dance can only --with apologies to Meredith Willson-- be imagined:

"Why, sisters, you've got Trouble with a capital T!"

"Where! Where!"

"Right here at St. Bernard's!"

"Lord! Lord!"

"These kids can't tap dance and it's a Sin! Yes, I say Sin with a capital S!"

Maybe it was the mention of Sin that did it.

Everyone was told to bring a quarter to school for the first mass tap-dancing lesson.

The classes were marched to the school hall where we stood in neat ranks by class for our first lesson. What we learned for our quarters that day was how to walk toe-to-heel and then heel-to-toe.

Platoons of kids thundered around the hall for a half-hour.

The experience would later help me understand Maoism.

Then we were given papers telling about the tap shoes everyone needed to order from the Dancing Man if we wanted to continue tap dance lessons. I don't recall there being a second mass tap-dancing lesson.

That was the only dancing lesson I had in my youth and high school dances later were rough affairs for me because I only knew how to tap dance. I could toe-heel and heel-toe through a fast number like "Peggy Sue," but tapping fell flat as a way of moving to a slow song like "Sixteen Candles" when you had to put your arm around the girl. I drank a lot of orange Tru-Ade in gym lobbies during teen dances. But I fared better than the guys who only knew how to play the piano a little.

It has not been easy fighting the great fight of life armed only with a 25-cent tap dance lesson.

With the thought of learning a new step and getting ahead in life, I took a free square dance lesson not long ago in the parking lot of a farm store out in the country during a squash festival or some such thing. A square dance club was giving a demonstration and soliciting volunteers to show how easy it is to learn to square dance.

One of the women in the group who wore a gaudy skirt with a hundred starched ruffles said, "I can tell you've had dancing lessons before," as I warmed up with a little toe-heel and heel-toe. My kids ran and hid.

As I told the woman about the nuns and the Dancing Man, it occurred to me that the group might conclude its demonstration by passing out papers saying you had to order cowboy boots and skirts with ruffles from them if you wanted to learn more about square dancing. But this didn't happen.

I was surprised at how easy it was to learn to square dance.

I threw my head back and my mind reeled with thoughts of what I might learn next --the Peppermint Twist, the Quadrille, the Boomps-a-Daisy. Success would be mine in the great dance of life.

But after the music stopped, I just bought a bag of squash and went home. And I never did get around to learning all those other dances.

The multi-talented people of the future will waltz through life, I imagine. Like others of my generation, I seem to move ahead very slowly, toe-to-heel, heel-to-toe.

Often, it doesn't even look like I am dancing.

# GUILT WITH MUSTARD

I was never as fond of home hot dogs as I was of stadium hot dogs when I was a kid.

Bloated and cracked in the pot, home hot dogs would float like ravaged submarines in steaming after-battle water and leak vital fluids that collected in oily lily pads on the surface.

They were not, to me, the same fare as Red Hots neatly pulled from a silver box by a vendor at Memorial Stadium.

Whenever my mother would fork a boiled hot dog onto a bun and hand it to me for lunch, my father would look down the table and say, "Make believe you are at the ballpark."

At that time my imagination must have been as weak as my appetite. I was never able to transform the wallpapered dining room of our house in Baynesville into the bleachers at the stadium. It was always a source of fascination to me that my father, a very serious man, was sitting at the far end of the table waiting for the next pitch whenever we had hot dogs.

It irritated my father that although I balked at eating home hot dogs, I would want a Red Hot whenever we were at the stadium. He would do some quick calculating and tell me how many hot dogs he could buy at the store and how many people he could feed for the price of one Red Hot. He would most often have me settle for a bag of peanuts.

I also yearned for Washington hot dogs that were sold then from carts along the mall on Constitution Avenue at the foot of the steps to every great building. In all fairness to my father, he did buy me a few stadium hot dogs because it is part of the American way, I guess. But he would never pay the high price for a Washington hot dog. Among the bits of advice he imparted as I was growing up was, "Never spend a nickel in Washington."

My father was not a patient man and he suffered from his relationship with me with what he called "aggravation."

"We'll eat when we get home," he would say to my countless pleas for a Washington hot dog every time we entered or left a building. Then he would talk about Washington, hot dog carts and the "aggravation" of it all.

"Someday, he'll have children of his own and find out what it's like," my mother would say.

It seemed to me that the single source of consolation my parents had when raising me was that somewhere down the line the tables would turn. I, of course, vowed that this would never happen and that my children would have all the hot dogs they wanted.

But I grew to learn that it is the secret nature of all tables to turn.

"Never spend a nickel in Washington," I wisely cautioned my family in the car on our most recent trip to Washington.

"That sounds like one of your father's sayings," my wife said.

She has learned the sound of my father's sayings: Never eat out when you have food at home; Never waste money on parking lots; Never be too proud to carry a lunch box no matter where you are going. There are many more.

At the stadium once when the hot dog vendor walked by, my wife looked over the heads of the kids sitting between us and said, "That's the kind of thing my father never would buy."

I was thinking the same thought, too, but about my father.

We looked at the many people around us who were buying one thing after another at high prices from vendors. We were both overwhelmed with the rampant excesses of the crowd. It is my wife's theory that all these people had fathers like ours and were making up for it now.

Swept along with the crowd, I suppose, she and the kids bought hot dogs. I couldn't bring myself to buy one. I ate leftovers from the kids. All the little butt ends tasted to me like guilt with mustard.

The kids are actually pretty good about not wanting everything they see when they are out. On the Washington trip, for instance, they walked past all the colorful lunch-and-souvenir trucks parked along the mall.

I thought of all the visits I had made to Washington with my parents and of all the hot dogs I had wanted. It is curious that whenever it was that the table turned on me, I never felt it move. Some things happen as slowly and imperceptibly as the progress of nature.

"Never spend a nickel in Washington!" the kids said.

I was proud of them.

# YARD TURTLES

Now it has rained turtles and, in turtle measure, poured.

During the last few weeks we have found four turtles in the woods beyond the house and have brought them into our yard. For almost a decade we had searched out there for turtles and never found even one.

That a backyard needs a turtle is a notion I acquired from the very old neighborhood in Baltimore where we lived when I was a small child.

The old people who lived there waxed, scrubbed, painted trimwork, swept away puddles after rainfalls and kept brown-and-yellow box turtles in their backyards.

The yards of the old people had bird baths. Their little lawns were manicured like putting greens. The wire fences gleamed with ever-fresh coats of silver paint, and a carefully shaped mound of coffee grounds was at the base of every evenly-spaced rose bush.

In the evenings the old people would water lawns, refill bird baths and squirt down their paths with green hoses. Their paths never were dirty, it seemed to me, but this is what they did.

I would walk the alley in the evening and stop outside the fences to look for the turtles that became active when the lawns and flower beds were watered. It is the way of the low-lying box turtle to wander when it rains.

Sometimes the old people, knowing what I was looking for, would go hunting among the marigolds and petunias for a turtle to show me. "This is a big one" or "Here's an old guy," they would say as they set a turtle on the wet path by the gate to the alley. The shell of the turtle would scrape lightly on the water-browned concrete as it moved away.

My great-aunt, who lived deeper in the city, kept turtles, too, in the small walled yard behind her house. I was left to spend an afternoon with her once and I followed her about the house all day as she cleaned with German precision and spoke to me in broken English. Her work was not finished that day until she found and lined in a row every turtle from the garden and gave each a shower from the hose and a brisk scrubbing with a long-handled brush. She had something to say to each turtle about how dirty it was.

Then she turned the nozzle on the hose to a fine spray and the turtles opened their shells and held their reptilian heads up in the rain.

"Are you supposed to do that to turtles?" I asked.

"The duddles like it," she said.

It was from my great-aunt's husband that we later obtained a few turtles for our own yard. Uncle seemed to have the ability to put his hat on in the morning, go to work in the heart of Baltimore and come home with turtles.

When we moved eventually from the city, we took our yard turtles with us. In the new neighborhood where all the people were young, only one other family kept turtles and very few people came out after it rained to sweep away puddles.

Our turtles had free run of the yard. They took triangular bites from slices of bologna I held in my hand and drank rain water from a section of concrete gutter at the wall of the house that didn't drain properly.

Whatever became of those yard turtles, I can't remember.

I think I am more pleased with the four turtles that we have just found than my kids are. I have fed them every imaginable kind of table scrap. Perhaps even more turtles will come our way when word gets out that a turtle can get a good meal of minute-steak and melon balls at my house.

The other day I lined the turtles on the driveway and squirted them lightly with the hose. They withdrew into their shells at once. I looked at each turtle carefully. The turtle preceded man on earth by 200 million years and evolved to its present form in the days of the dinosaur. I have always envied the silence and serenity of the box turtle. I think it comes from the security of the shell and the fact that they have no ears and are deaf.

As I adjusted the nozzle on the hose to a fog-fine primeval mist, the turtles slowly emerged from their shells. In this ancient aura they stretched their necks and looked about alertly.

In the spirit of celebrating a yesterday, I bent down and rubbed at the dirt on their shells with my hand.

# SIGNS AND THEIR TIMES

The Bloop Ball was once a popular novelty. It is a styrofoam baseball weighted off-center so that a simple throw produces curves and erratic bloops.

My older boy and a friend were playing with one in the yard, and I wondered where they got it. I recalled a dim image of playing with one when I was a kid as I watched from the kitchen window. It was cold and they didn't play long. The neighbor boy had no interest in the ball (his father had just given it to him), and he gave it to my son who brought it into the house and deposited it on the kitchen counter, a sort of Ellis Island, unfortunately for my wife, for all things entering the house that no one knows where to put.

As I tossed the ball from hand to hand, I noticed that it carried a small circular stamp: METER CLUB, ORIOLES, 1959. The first three letters of the name of the club are partially obliterated, though the first one seems to be either an S or a G. I would speculate confidently that the ball was a commemorative item of the Gasmeter Club, except that the fragment of the second letter, a little black mark, doesn't seem to be in a place where it could be any part of an A.

I felt a bit like Sherlock Holmes as I studied the surface of the ball: A foul crime had been committed and Lestrade had brought me the only clue to be found at the scene --a Bloop Ball.

As I further examined the surface of the ball, I discovered inkless impressions that appeared to be bits of handwriting. I covered one of them with paper and rubbed lightly with the side of a pencil point, but all I got was a smear of black. The impressions were faint and the ball was nicked and pitted.

I gave up on this approach after three attempts, and I then scrutinized a fragment using a variety of light angles until I got: a-- -ich. I worked on a second fragment: eb-ban.

The ball was a quarter-century old and I was fascinated with it.

It didn't take me long to surmise that the two inscriptions were autographs: Paul Richards and Weeb Ewbank. What Colt coach Ewbank was doing at an Oriole affair, I don't know. But I can imagine a father-and-son night at a sports club featuring keg beer, pickle-and-pimento loaf sandwiches and ballplayers signing autographs.

I thought I had found all the writing on the ball (and I was about to ring for Mrs. Hudson to bring me some Doritos and a Tab) when I came upon what seemed to be a $y$ sitting by itself. This signature was almost invisible: --- l-y G--s.

This had to be the autograph of Bailey Goss, the Baltimore sportscaster during the early days of television when most of a game was covered by a single camera up and behind home plate.

I can remember being taken long ago by my father to father-and-son sports nights in a church basement. It was fun to be out at night, among men drinking beer and smoking cigars, and getting Oriole and Colt autographs.

I dug out my autograph book from the mid-Fifties from a trunk in the basement. There were not many names: Billy Hunter, Joe Coleman, Bob Kennedy, Bo Bo Newsom, Chuck Thompson, Tom Gastall, Dean Renfro, Jim Mutscheller, Royce Womble, Ken Jackson, Cotton Davidson, Art Donovan, Johnny Unitas, George Preas, Dick Young. I never developed into a sports fan and most of the names hold no memories or have no meaning for me. But for some readers, the names will be nostalgic.

As I was rummaging through the trunk, I discovered a collection of mementoes of days I had forgotten. There was a crumpled high school class tie of hideous gold with three horizontal red stripes. It had to be worn by freshmen until Christmas, unless the Cardinals beat the Dons at the stadium on Thanksgiving morning. I can't remember what happened. I also found a ridiculous gray and green cap I had to wear on campus as a college freshman. I can't recall how long the freshmen had to wear the caps. I am not sure why the ugly tie and the silly hat have been saved. But I supposed it has to do with holding on to time.

A few summers ago on a hot day, I stood in line with the older boy for several hours at the Crown station in Bel Air to get Brooks Robinson's autograph. I had plenty of time to ponder the meaning of what I was doing. I realized that I was spending almost three hours of my life on Earth in the galaxy Milky Way waiting for a man to write his name on a baseball.

I am not sure of the value or significance of autographs. For some, autographs are cherished possessions --a way of holding onto time and even onto a person. But the lesson of the Bloop Ball has to do with transience and, I think, that so much of life is written in styrofoam.

# WHITE T-SHIRTS

I associate the white T-shirt with hot summer evenings and childhood memories of real men.

I see Uncle John at the table with an ever-present Chesterfield and cup of coffee telling firehouse stories (he would die at a fire); Uncle Jack sitting before a mountain of mashed potatoes, his steel-mill arms stretching the sleeves of his T-shirt; my dad and Uncle Alvin in the alley changing brake shoes on a Studebaker; Mr. Lee sitting on his back porch working with a pencil in his milkman's book; Mr. Mincher, home from a stint on the railroad, waxing his car.

The white T-shirt was what was left when the blue collar came off at the end of a hot day.

No one had air conditioners in the old neighborhood and the heat in the houses was terrible, which is why, I suppose, men wore only undershirts at home. The nearby drugstore, which had large windows and heavy glass doors that dripped with condensation, was the only place I recall being air-conditioned. A decal on a window of a penguin standing on an ice cake touted, "It's Kool Inside."

I could not pass the drugstore, my first encounter with air conditioning, without entering to walk aisles aimlessly, not believing that in summer there was a place that felt and smelled as clean as winter.

Then a few neighbors purchased window fans to draw a hot draft through selectively opened windows, but my father decided it would be cheaper to build a window fan than to buy one, a decision that sorely aggrieved my mother.

An old washing machine motor was the heart of his fan. He built a plywood box, many times larger than a commercial window fan, painted it gray with leftover porch paint, and mounted the washing machine motor, a store-bought blade and a conglomeration of shafts and belts. But he installed two pulleys backwards.

When he tested it in the basement, the box roared like a factory machine, flew in several bounds across the floor and sent the assembled crowd of onlookers, including my mother, running for their lives. The Wright brothers would have been impressed.

But my mother was not pleased. Nevertheless, my father reversed the pulleys, nailed on two grills of rabbit wire and installed the contraption in the dining-room window. Because of its size, furniture was rearranged. My mother declared the fan a disgrace and said no one could ever be invited into our house again.

Summer nights before the fan had been miserable. I lay coverless in bed and perspired. I smelled scented soap from the bathroom and heated attic insulation. As heat lightning flashed, an ill baby across the alley cried night after night. In later years, Mr. Lee would help me get a milkman's job. I delivered milk before dawn on summer mornings in similar neighborhoods of row houses where I would find men in white T-shirts sleeping in chairs, women and children tumbled on mattresses on the porches. If a man stirred as I approached, he usually asked what time it was. As the truck growled about in the dark, I nurtured a sense of the universality of my childhood blue-collar images, finding in them something celebratory, too:

"This is the carol of occupations," wrote Whitman. "In the labor of engines and trades...I find the developments, and find the eternal meanings."

My father's fan worked well, and thereafter on hot summer nights the house would be closed except for the bedroom windows which were opened only slightly. Cool air streamed over the beds. From my window I saw shadows of men here and there on back porches in the dark, their white T-shirts glowing in moonlight, languid red dots from cigarettes appearing then like fireflies --and in mind now as distant beacons.

# SCHOOL FIGURES

# STARTING AN ORANGE

After teaching high school for 18 years, my appointment to a middle school brought some surprises.

As a high school teacher I dealt mainly with juniors and seniors who often towered above me, looked like adults and, quite often, behaved like adults. It was easy to forget that I was dealing with children. Teenagers just don't look like "children." And high school teachers tend to think of themselves as teachers of English, math, history, and science.

But in a middle school there is no mistaking that a teacher is a teacher of children. On the first day of school my eyes were opened as I stood by the door of a sixth-grade classroom. It was culture shock for me. I had spent almost 20 years looking a foot overhead at Rambo-type boys in motorcycle jackets. Now I felt like Gulliver in Lilliput.

I spent my first few days in middle school wandering about in a daze. I was as bewildered as the incoming sixth graders who were having fits trying to learn how to work the combination locks on their lockers.

I had thought that students were born with an instinctive ability to operate combination locks, but this is not so. During the first week of school I walked the hall with other teachers and waved my arms in the air as the kids imitated to demonstrate clockwise and counter-clockwise. A visitor would have thought that we were teaching the sixth grade how to fly.

Among my duties was supervision of the sixth-grade lunch shift.

"Hey, Mr. Teacher!" a boy called.

"Yes?" I said as I approached the table.

"Will you start my orange?"

"What?" I said.

"Will you start my orange?" He held up an enormous orange.

"Just bite the skin a little," I said.

"I can't."

"Why not?" I asked.

"Braces," he said. He opened his mouth wide to prove it.

It really was a tough orange. When I succeeded in breaking the skin, my thumb shot all the way into the orange.

"Thanks," the boy said.

It was the first time in my career that I had been asked to start an orange.

During those early days I had to struggle to grasp my new identity. I walked about the cafeteria contemplating my sticky thumb.

One day I took a class on a field trip to Baltimore to tour the Pratt Library and the Walters Art Gallery. On the bus I learned all the words to a television commercial song about how if you eat all the chocolate morsels off your cookie, the cookie will be bald. The song doesn't have many words and I mastered it between the Jones Falls Expressway and Cathedral Street. I discovered that I was enjoying myself very much.

From the bus window I looked at all the business people walking about. I wondered where they were going. I also wondered about how I spend my days.

At the library, we left behind a constellation of noseprints on the locked glass door to the Poe Room. As I stood back, I thought it was a wonderful sight. I studied the stars on the glass and felt an intimation of a sense of direction in my new world.

I also had an opportunity to chaperon a middle school dance. "Dance" is not the right word. I am reminded of the scene when Macbeth asks the witches on the heath what they are doing and they reply, "A deed without a name."

Within an hour the air in the cafeteria was locker-room damp and the windows fogged. When parents arrived to pick up their kids they said, "My!" as they peeped in to the cafeteria. Some of the more eloquent said, "Oh, my!"

I believe I had more fun than I ever had chaperoning high school dances and proms. But I am not sure why.

As the months have passed I have come to regard myself more as a teacher of children than a teacher of English. I am also nurturing a paradoxical perception that being a teacher, even though teachers are paid poorly, may actually be a privilege, and I find myself thinking that I am lucky to be a teacher.

I was apprehensive about leaving high school, but sometimes you put in a thumb and pull out a plum.

Or an orange.

# THRILLS OF THE REAL WORLD

Once, when *The Evening Sun* was running a series of articles on public education in Baltimore, a blunt headline appeared on the front page which declared that teachers are boring their students.

As a teacher and a journalist, I felt a double responsibility to look further into the matter. I spent many weeks studying the situation. And I am afraid it is true that many of my teaching colleagues are not sufficiently entertaining their classes.

Teachers seem wholly oblivious to the fact that in addition to saying "Let there be light" and "Go forth and multiply," the voice that spoke over the waters also said, "Let the good times roll." Teachers don't seem to know what life is all about.

Too many teachers have let their acts go to ruin. I have seen teachers appear before their classes with their fright-wigs on crooked and their seltzer bottles half empty. I have seen teachers attempt to get through a 50-minute class with only a 15-minute supply of confetti. And I guess I am as guilty as the rest. It has been years since I taught my dancing bear a new step or oiled the propeller on my beanie.

Yes, teachers are boring their classes and as a result, great masses of 18-year-olds are sent into the world each June thoroughly unprepared to cope with the excitement of reality.

I recently attended the five-year reunion of a class I had taught and listened attentively as a number of them glumly played with the cherries in their whiskey sours and talked about the problems they were having adjusting to the thrills of the real world.

"Life is too much fun," a young man said. "I wasn't prepared for it. The schools aren't doing their jobs."

"I know what you mean," a young woman said. "You spend 12 years in school being bored to death with skills and concepts and then you step into the real world and find that life is one big blast. Employers aren't interested in your abilities. All they care about is whether or not you are capable of having a good time."

"I've been fired from two jobs since I graduated," another young fellow said. "They were too much fun and I didn't know how to handle myself. It's all the fault of the schools."

"I had this one job," a second young woman said, "where the boss would come into the office at the beginning of the day with a big smile and say, 'Let me entertain you.' He would sort of sing it and shuffle his feet. Then he would tell us about all the fun things he had in store for us that day. I would break down and cry. After being bored in school for 12 years, I couldn't take the shock. I quit."

"Come now," I said as I looked around the table. "Didn't some of your teachers try to entertain you?"

There was a silence. Finally, the guy sitting next to me said, "Maybe."

"Wasn't there a biology teacher at our school who used to juggle gerbils?" someone said.

"I remember him," the guy next to me said. "He wasn't any good at it. He had no business being in a classroom."

"What about the lady who taught history in a bikini and used to draw maps on her stomach with a ballpoint pen?" someone recalled.

"Yeah, but she couldn't stay on her unicycle," a voice said.

"I remember that math teacher who would accept an answer as long as it was close," someone said. "But he was still boring. That seal of his couldn't play a tune for beans."

"Well, what about that song-and-dance number the women in the English department whipped up about sentence structure?" I asked. "Do you remember the good part: *You'll learn how a sentence functions--when we shake our conjunctions*," I weakly sang.

"Yeah," the guy next to me said, "but they kept dropping their canes."

What I discovered during my study was an entertainment gap as wide as the generation gap. I don't know what it will take to close it.

It is a depressing situation when teachers cannot provide their classes with the kind of fun they need to be prepared for life.

# DEATH IN THE AFTERNOON

Willy Loman always dies in the heat near the end of May. It's the order of the curriculum. Then Hemingway's Santiago, the old man who fought the marlin, must die. After these two are bumped off, the 11th-graders can go home for their summer vacation.

The kids who attend school regularly at this time of year --when it's too hot to think and everyone has had it-- deserve a pat on their wet backs.

"Why does Willy Loman kill himself?" I always ask.

"He was too hot to care anymore," is the answer I get most years.

I turned out the classroom lights to make it seem cooler on the afternoon we were to learn that Biff really did steal the basketballs. The hair I had carefully fluffed over a thin spot that morning at home was a sparse mat of wet strings.

In the dark, through the wet, dead air, Lee J. Cobb shouted the grief and madness of Willy Loman out of the mouth of a record player. I watched with my mean and nasty teacher eyes to see that all the pages in the copies of "Death of a Salesman" turned when they should as the record played. Three kids didn't turn their pages when the others did. I wondered what they were dreaming. Behind the death ray of my gaze, I dreamed of my air-conditioned house and a can of cold beer.

A car crawled along the drive in front of the school. Loud music came from the car. The driver succeeded in attracting the attention of a thousand people. Lee J. Cobb was raving for the attention of 25 of them.

Within minutes, two other cars came racing out of the parking lot in a passion of blatting exhaust, hot squealing wheels and four speakers' worth of a rock number that featured guitars, drums and a lot of screaming. These two cars also succeeded in commanding the attention of a thousand people. Lee J. Cobb yelled in the darkness to the four walls as Willy Loman moved toward his death. The rock group screamed back at him from the road as the cars pulled away.

It could be worse. It was fashionable last year to pull dad's car up in front of the school and stand on the brake and accelerator simultaneously for as long as a minute. The front brakes would hold the car in place, but the back wheels would break free and generate thick clouds of smoke as they spun in place.

The smoking effect could be enhanced if you spilled laundry bleach under the rear tires. Much more smoke could be made if you used bleach. I don't know why. Many did this. Last year when Willy Loman was dying, two cars having a contest on the main road in front of the school made so much smoke that traffic was brought to a standstill.

On the afternoon we were to learn that Biff really did steal the basketballs, the record kept playing. At their desks, some kept wiping themselves with coarse brown paper towels they had taken from the top drawer of my filing cabinet on the way into the room. Amenities are few. You get a book, a chair and a paper towel.

A girl turned a red smear of a face up to me and mouthed, "It's too hot." The water running down her arms looked yellow. I mouthed back, "I know." I smiled. She knew that I believed her; it was all she wanted. She looked back into her book. She was about to find out that Biff really did steal the basketballs.

Then a groundsman came with a tractor and began to mow the grass by the windows. The din was terrific. The record turned round and round but no sound could be heard from the speaker. The tractor went back and forth. The lawn mower ate Willy Loman. It ate Happy and Biff. It ate the basketballs. It was all over.

On a hot afternoon before this, a sudden cloudburst with wind and thunder ate all the sentences we were writing that were packed with appositive, participial and absolute phrases. The class worked hard despite the heat. A boy raised his hand to read his sentence and as he opened his mouth lightning flashed and thunder ate his sentence. We saw his lips move, but we heard nothing.

Then the rain came in wildly flapping sheets of silver and the wind began to drive the heat from the room. There were only a few minutes left in the school day. I raised the blinds to the ceiling and we watched the rain like thirsty people.

Suddenly, a boy on a bicycle appeared down below on the sidewalk in front of the school. He had his shirt off and he was riding with only the rear wheel of the bike on the ground. The front wheel was high in the air and the boy's head was thrown back as he quickly passed. He rode right through the rain, wind and thunder. I was the only one who saw him because I had made the class stay in their chairs. The boy looked like the luckiest person who had ever lived. It would have tortured the class to see him.

The class had thrown their damp heads down on their desks. Their eyes were closed. They could feel the wind better that way, I guess. It was the death of a school day.

# SUCKLING'S FLIGHT

I recently spent two weeks in a think tank.

The large building with broad, open spaces was conducive to thinking large thoughts. And it was cool --too downright frigid for some-- inside the carpeted caverns with two-story ceilings that glowed from hidden lights. The lighting was muted in the large rooms, the passageways dim, and, with the carpet muffling sound, the atmosphere was a perpetual twilight --or of what life would be like on a great space ship moving silently, as gentle music played, outward bound.

There were no windows and neither the heat of July nor even a sense of time of day ever entered the building as it hummed serenely, coldly forward.

Once a rumble of thunder was heard and someone cried out like a ship's captain, "Storm's coming! Better Save, boys!" Keys quickly clicked on word processors to Save --record on tape-- the contents of computer memories before a power failure cleared them, and a whole morning's work would be lost. But everything was Saved and the great silent thinking ship was ready for the storm.

Someone pushed open a heavy door to the outside, and like Huck and Jim sitting in the mouth of their cave on Jackson's island watching a summer storm (one of Twain's finest descriptive passages), we watched the approaching storm until the first rain came splattering. All that was missing was the hot catfish and corn bread. When the door was closed, the sound of the storm disappeared completely. Keys clicked again. My partner and I worked at a table facing a white wall to minimize distractions. No catfish. No corn bread.

It was our job to write a portion of a new 12th-grade English curriculum. We were to revise and further develop a pilot unit of study on Elizabethan literature written last summer and to expand the unit to cover the entire Renaissance. We had two weeks to write about 30 pages of objectives and activities for students of varying abilities with a balance of language, composing and interpreting experiences. I was one of about 400 Baltimore County public school teachers, drawn from many disciplines, who gathered at Pine Grove Middle School to write curriculum.

One of the requirements of curriculum writing is that objectives must be written to include a purpose. For instance: "Students will read and view 'Macbeth' to...". Now what is needed is a purpose. Think about it. Exactly why should students read "Macbeth?" Then you have to develop assessable exercises that will achieve that purpose for students of varying abilities.

Two weeks of asking why can undermine your faith in the meaning of life if you get carried away: Exactly why should a 17-year-old wearing a *GRAB A HEINE*! T-shirt dramatize in modern English Christopher Marlowe's and Sir Walter Raleigh's companion poems "The Passionate Shepherd to His Love" and "The Nymph's Reply to the Shepherd?"

And there are other decisions: Given that the minimum daily adolescent requirement of sonnets is zero, how can the Renaissance be covered without doing permanent damage to the students' minds? Is Sir Thomas Wyatt really worth it? Will Richard (snicker) Lovelace work? Will Sir John (snicker-snicker) Suckling fly? Right out the window, probably.

And other work tables had similar concerns. The Victorian table debated racism in *Tarzan of the Apes*. The Romantic table worked to protect students from poetry burnout. The Modern table agonized over dropping the close reading of Dylan Thomas' "Fern Hill" for something easier, such as T.S. Elliot's "Preludes". A table with no name --working on activities for an opening unit on "Oedipus Rex" and the Bible as Literature-- cast about for an identity. They were not the Foundations of British Literature, as the pilot indicated. Nor were they the Origins as someone suggested. Finally they became the Classic Heritage. Behind my post at the Renaissance table, the Medieval table was challenged to devise a way of teaching the "Canterbury Tales" with a text containing only the prologue and one tale. (I, myself, see nothing wrong with teaching the "Canterbury Tale" and being done with it.)

When it was over, I headed straight for the ocean with my family to camp out in the living room of a relative's rented condominium. Within hours of the close of the curriculum workshop I was walking in the surf. Gratefully, I felt the Renaissance begin to wash away. After two intense weeks in the cool, white, silent think tank, I found myself muttering, "Yes, there is a natural world." My eyes, so used to focusing on print at the distance of a foot, struggled to comprehend the expanse of the ocean.

As I stood in the surf, two teenagers wearing the then popular *PARTY NAKED* T-shirts passed by on the beach. I shopped that night for a T-shirt that said *READ JOHN DONNE NAKED* --or something like that.

Didn't find one.

# THE BLACK-ROBED WIZARDS

At podiums under the arc of the firmament they stand at the cusp of spring and summer. Though skies vary from swirls of damp and nervous gray fuzz to domes of white-hot metal, they always find something wise to say about the weather.

They are good at their job. They are, after all, commencement speakers:

"Though the wind bends the great trees above us, and a storm has come which will probably make mincemeat of this commencement, I am sure that we are all really looking toward the future."

Yes, commencement speakers in their borrowed wizard-black robes with colored hoods perform their annual magic. They dutifully invoke the old names and resurrect the likes of Plato, Shakespeare, and Abraham Lincoln before audiences which are thinking of cold beer and the pounds of salami that await them at home.

But the speakers are applauded for their services. No commencement would be complete without a commencement speaker. Schools may wise up some day and get people like Cheryl Tiegs or Wonder Woman to speak.

Commencement speakers talk mostly about yesterday and tomorrow. Few speak of today, except in a general way. ("I am delighted to be here today.") I think it's because today is too chancey a topic. They might make a mistake.

The past is a safe topic for commencement speakers because everyone pretty much agrees on what happened during the last ice age, the Korean middle ages, the Renaissance.

And the handful of invited guests who know what is going to happen in the future are usually too busy preparing for it by drinking wine and renting sailboats to accept graduation invitations. They tend to send greeting cards and checks to graduates along with their regrets. Their absence makes the future a safe topic for commencement speakers, also.

During this commencement season, many a notable arm trailing a yard of black silk will wave in one direction where they think the past is. They will point out the mistakes of yesterday.

Then, with a passing on-center thump or two of the podium that counts as an acknowledgment of today, they will flap owl wings to the other direction and talk about the future.

Speakers at graduations always seem to think that they are sending the youths who endure them into the future. But, as we all know, graduates tend to scatter with their scrolls in all directions after the procession ends in an alley behind a field house or in a parking lot by a garage where these groundskeepers park the lawn mowers.

Why graduates scatter in all directions is because commencement speakers often forget that when they wave into the future, the audience --with its reversed perspective-- interprets the signal as a charge to depart campus in the opposite direction, that is into the past.

Some of my old friends went into the past. They send me cards postmarked "Mesopotamia," "Dark Ages," and "Wild West." They seem to be having a good time, though. I can only assume that old colleagues who never write went into the future.

There are many hills from which you can see distant things. But what the future holds for any class is hard to tell unless you know the right hill to climb.

People often speak of hills so high that you can "see from here to Christmas." Most of us have climbed such hills and have seen Christmas. There are other, even higher hills from which people claim you can "see clear around the world." I suppose you would see the back of your own head from those hills.

But hills from which you can see the future are hard to find. Cynics, who have been there and back, say you can only see more of the same. They say it's like looking into a mirror. But you seldom hear a pessimistic commencement speaker: "It's a pleasure to be here, but all of you kids are doomed."

Most commencement speakers are optimistic about the future. They claim to have seen something better from the peaks of the secret hills they know and their owl wings point to tomorrow.

I'm not sure who is right this commencement season, but I would still rather hear about it from Cheryl Tiegs.

# FINDING OUT

When I was a teenager, I never had conversations with my parents. We mostly had arguments.

The arguments that passed for conversations would usually end in a thunderous finale of frustration when either my mother or father would shout, "Someday, you'll find out!"

Whenever my mother delivered the closing line, she would gesture dramatically like an actress in a Greek tragedy. My father would just beat his fist on the kitchen table like a judge rapping down a gavel after sentencing someone to death.

It seemed as if the only way my parents were ever going to get revenge on me adequately for all the grief I was bringing them by being a normal teenager was by turning me over to the cruel hands of the future.

A few years ago, a girl wearing a green summer dress asked a very special question in my classroom during the last week of school.

"Is there something we don't know?" she asked. "People are always saying, 'Someday, you'll find out.' Is there something we haven't been told? Is there a secret we are going to find out after we graduate?"

Everyone turned their eyes from her to me. The question floated toward me on a sea of silence. On the flat surface of the water I saw the face of my mother, the face of my father.

I paused to gauge the depth of the silence and the importance of the moment.

"Yes," I finally said. "There are a few secrets."

I paused again. On the clock above me, the red hand moved hotly.

Then the girl in the green dress whispered in a breeze-like voice in the hushed room. "Tell us," she said.

I thought for a moment and then I did. I said that most of the good you find in life comes from self-sacrifice; that you have to develop a view of life that can accommodate loss and sorrow; that true love is hard work; that the most beautiful things in life come mostly in moments as small as a grain of sand.

The class sighed with relief as I spoke. The tension was broken. They had heard all this before. There really was no secret you only got to know when you turned a certain age.

"We thought you were going to tell us something important," a boy said. He was disappointed, I guess, that I hadn't told the class that we were aliens and that we were going to return to our home planet in 1996 or something like that.

But the girl in the green dress who had been brave enough to ask the dangerously self-revealing question gave me the greatest compliment I have ever received as a teacher. She looked at me very seriously. Then she smiled and said, "I knew you would tell the truth." It was a moment as small as a grain of sand.

Now it is time for this class to cultivate a small moment. The time has come to feel a goodbye.

This last assembly before commencement gives farewell a form. But each of you should shape a private goodbye.

In the opening pages of J.D. Salinger's *The Catcher in the Rye*, with which this class is familiar, Holden Caulfield stood on a hill on a cold afternoon looking down on a school he was leaving.

The letter telling his parents that he had been expelled from Pencey Prep, a boarding school for boys, was already in the mail. He was standing on the hill looking down at the school because, as he put it, he was "trying to feel some kind of good-by."

Holden stood on the hill on a bleak December day until he recalled how once when he was throwing a football around with two friends and it was getting darker and darker, a friendly teacher raised a window and told them to go to their dorm and get ready for dinner. That memory gave Holden his feeling of goodbye, and he ran down from the hill.

I am not sure how Holden got a feeling of goodbye from that memory. But as a possible explanation, I offer a line from a letter written in 1903 by the Austrian poet Rainer Maria Rilke to a youth seeking advice.

"Things are not all so comprehensible and expressible," Rilke wrote, "as one would mostly have us believe; most events of personal importance are inexpressible, taking place in a realm which no word has ever entered."

I hope that you look on the shore of memory for something small as you try to feel a goodbye. I hope that you find something and feel something that would be hard to explain to anyone else.

If you expect more out of life than the joy that comes in small private moments, if you expect more than the secret dignity that comes from shouldering responsibility and sorrow, you may well be crushed under the weight of your own disappointment.

Turn pain into wisdom and turn love into more love. I think that is what my parents were trying to tell me by word and deed when I was young.

When did the big Someday come when I finally Found Out?

It began a long time ago. It's still going on. And I have a suspicion that Someday is as long as your life.

# A LIGHT SENTENCE

# OF ANGELS, AND PINHEADS

They wait sphinx-like where nothingness is something. They are philosophers, gentlemen who can mix a gin-dry question with the perfect sniff of vermouth: "Tell us now, does the light in the refrigerator really go out when you close the door?" Then the pause before the fall of the single, silvery orb of vermouth: "Can you prove that it does?"

For this I lived to be 18, I thought when I was in college. For four years I suffered the riddles (if your canary dies while you're asleep, is he really dead?) and vowed revenge.

Often in the old days in philosophy class --sixteen major building-fund drives ago according to my mail from the alumni office-- I felt like one of the children at the parade in the Hans Christian Anderson story where the emperor shows off his new clothes but is actually marching in the buff. At the parade, the adults admired the nonexistent clothes sold to the emperor by the crafty tailors who had used the emperor's vanity to work their scam. But the innocent children beheld the bare facts.

One day when I had enough of trying to prove that the flagpole by the dean's office was really there, I raised my hand and said to the school's oldest philosopher, "Sir, I think you are quite naked."

He paused, obviously following neither my train of thought nor my allusion. "Like the emperor in the fairy tale," I quickly added.

"Can you prove it?" he asked. "You failed miserably when it came to the light bulb in the refrigerator last week. Now you are not very attentive to this business of the dean's flagpole."

I had a feeling my sophomoric gambit was about to be ground into relish.

"And if I recall correctly," he continued, "last year as a freshman, you skirted the issue of whether a falling tree in the Black Forest makes a sound when there is no one present to hear it by citing a German forester --whose book you have yet to place in my hand-- who claimed that trees do not fall in the Black Forest because of the climate. So you wish to prove that I am naked? All I say is, Ha!" He had me there. Ha! is historically the most difficult argument to counter. You have to know how to say it.

That was many years ago. I never thought of getting even, but as recently as last week my wife caught me kneeling at the refrigerator and peeking through the crack as I slowly closed the door. "I can't take any more of this," she said. "Why don't you just call that old professor and ask him for an answer?" But I didn't have to. He came to me.

There was a letter from old alma mater asking for money to finance another building. This one was special. The old philosophy professor had been made chairman of this building-fund drive. Inside was a little return envelope just the size of a bank check. Instead of a check, I wrote a note to the old professor: "I would like to pay, no matter the cost, for putting up a flagpole by the dean's office. How much will it cost?"

A letter came back. I had him going. It said, "There has always been a flagpole by the dean's office and we are not in need of a new one. There are many other needs a contribution could fulfill."

"I always thought there was a flagpole by the dean's office," I said to my wife.

I tried again. The buried seed of revenge had come alive. I sent him another envelope with this note: "Enclosed is $10,000 in cold cash. Use it as you please."

He wrote back: "Thank you, but there was no money to be found in the envelope."

I wrote back: "Prove it."

He wrote back: "Ha!"

Like Oedipus before the Sphinx in the desert, I returned that night in the darkness to stand at the refrigerator. Every man must answer his own riddle on the road to Thebes. But I cannot help wishing I had gone to school when things were easier and you only had to hear the sound of one hand clapping.

# PUPPET PERIL

Somewhere in the engine of time and space, a gear has slipped. Puppets seem to be taking the country by storm. The lintlipped, dry-clean-only Muppets and the fur-and-feather cast of "Sesame Street" reign supreme.

Puppets sing and dance. They take our money and leave us laughing. But things have gone too far. We have sold our souls to a Punch-and-Judy mania that puts the great entrepreneurial joke of frozen pizza to shame.

Puppets have their own TV shows, movies and records. On the cover of a September issue of *People* magazine, the likes of Cheryl and Linda were bumped for a cheese-shot of that Herculon-harpy, Miss Piggy.

Is this what was meant by "Vive la difference"?

At the magazine rack by the checkout counter in the supermarket, a man pointed his dead cigar stub at the magazine cover featuring the porcine pulchritude of Miss Piggy. "She's a cutie," he said. "But she's too pink for me." He put the short piece of cigar back in his mouth. He lit it absently as he stared at Miss Piggy.

Folks have taken to little fiber-filled people with wide open arms and the band plays on. But not me. When people are out and puppets are in, I am afraid. Before me is a card from a reputable local theatre group. I am invited to a puppet production of "Hamlet." Surely, puppet productions of the classics are classic in themselves; but when the great Globe has gone to the talking socks, enough is enough.

I believe that Orwell's vision of the future may come in a form that outstrips our imagination. When I voice my fear of the Puppet Peril, I am poo-pooed by the best. "You never know," they say mockingly, "inside every great puppet is a hand."

But a man who knows the truth is a lonely man. It shows. When they see the look on my face, they get serious. "Hey," they whisper condescendingly, "they're just puppets."

When this and all else fail, they get nasty. They look at me sideways. "If that's the way you feel about puppets," they snarl, "go live among people."

"That's just what I am trying to do," I retort.

I fear humankind is doomed. Perhaps it's but the just fate of those who have looked too long at lavalights and desiccated their brains with blow-dyers.

We are victims of the Geppetto Syndrome: Puppets are becoming real. That is the problem. Two puppets, according to my children, are real: Ernie and Bert of "Sesame Street". I have not lost my perspective. I know, for instance, that Big Bird is not real. Nothing that yellow could be real. But Ernie and Bert are as real as Cheech and Chong, and Ham and Jody.

Neighborhood children who have seen "The Muppet Movie" have gone even further than my own kids. They tell me that every one in that movie is real except for Orson Welles, who appears briefly at the end.

"I seen him sniffing wine on TV," a little boy said disdainfully. "He's just a person."

"Weren't there a few other people in the movie?" I asked.

"There were some other guys," he admitted, "but they should have left them out. They ruined it."

With presidential elections every four years, I fear the puppets who chew the cherry at the top of the heap while the masses swoon to the tune of a banjo-picking, Kool-Aid-green frog. If puppets get involved in politics, the logical next step from show business, the end is nigh.

Any anarchist with a few of grandma's old cookie cutters could clone the "Saturday Night Live" doughboy, Mr. Bill, and bring us all to ruin. Save us also from an argyle-administration that would blame its flubs on the evil half pound of flour, salt, and water called Sluggo.

Whether puppet-fever is mere fun or the dangerous atavism of a latently totemistic culture, I do not know. The sky may not fall, but I am sure Chicken Little will have his own anthropomorphic last laugh.

# THE CHAIN-SAW BOYS

A tree fell in the yard, apparently of its own accord. Within minutes, three strange men appeared on the front porch. They wore puffy goose-down vests and were carrying chain saws. It was 6:30 on a Saturday morning.

As I opened the door, a collective voice seemed to say, "We are Tom, Dick and Harry. We live here and there in the neighborhood."

"I've never seen you guys before," I said.

"Yes, you have," my wife whispered over my shoulder. "You are the neighborhood joggers, aren't you?" she said to them.

"I didn't recognize you guys with clothes," I said.

"We recognize you," they said together with the perfect timing of a well trained Greek chorus and a trace of American barbershop harmony. "You used to stand at the front window as we jogged by and wave a can of suds and a fat salty pretzel at us."

"It was the best I could do," I said. "My mouth was always full of cheese."

"Well, all that's forgotten now," they said. "We were awakened from our deep, apple-wood scented sleeps by the sound of your falling tree. Because yours is the only house on the block which doesn't sport a newly built brick chimney, we came immediately."

"Thank you," I interrupted.

"Obviously," they continued as their chain-saws dripped oil onto the porch, "you have no need for the tree. We can cut it up and take it away in a matter of minutes. It's what we are into now."

They had a point. I told them to help themselves. I made coffee and watched from the kitchen window.

The three ex-joggers, now merrily clad in their lumberjack costumes, ran into the backyard and pulled away at the cords on their chainsaws. At first, the saws burped on the sudden flood of gasoline. Then they snarled and snapped, yelped and barked.

This was not my first encounter with fireplace people. A few weeks before, I attended a somewhat dressy affair at the home of a nouveau-fireplace person.

I stamped my freshly shined shoes to shake away the cold that night as I rang the bell. But when the door opened, the wave of heat which almost blew me off the porch was oppressive.

The host, a cheery man with a damp red face, reached out quickly and pulled me into the oven.

"How's that for heat," he said. "I've already melted down one fireplace grate this winter and I think this one has only a few hours left."

I shaded my eyes as I gazed at the fire.

Later, a log rolled from the top of the wildly popping inferno. It sat burning in the middle of the carpet. I sat transfixed with a broken chip and a knuckle full of dip.

A stately women with bluish hair at whose feet the log lay burning said, "Oh, piffle."

She dashed a glass of champagne onto the log in the manner common to ladies dismissing audacious suitors in roadhouses.

The host found two places on the log that were miraculously not aflame. He snatched the errant hunk of oak. With great aplomb, he returned it to its proper place.

These were real fireplace-people. No one in the room seemed the least bit ruffled. Not a single singed eyebrow was raised. The genial ambiance, which was comparable to that of the engine room of an old coalburning steamship, prevailed.

"More wood, more wood!" my host cried to his son. The boy ran outside and passed logs through the dining room window into his father's waiting arms.

The three lumberjacks in my yard had made quick work of it and were finishing up when I saw one of them eye the redwood benches by the picnic table. I rapped sharply on the window glass with a coffee spoon.

As they left the yard with their booty, I lowered the window. "If those benches should ever die and fall over in the night, I'll let you know," I said.

"Don't worry," they said. "We'll hear them."

A few hours later, another lumberjack rang the bell. I could tell he was a novice. His chain-saw sat at his feet in an unopened box. A price tag dangled from his puffy vest. The mortar in his fireplace was probably still damp.

"Am I too late?" he asked. "I'm new at this."

"I'm new at this, too," I said.

# JUST A LITTLE HEART

Was it radioactive milk or was it something in the winds of time that turned Raggedy Ann into Barbie?

War toys were recently banned in Sweden and at the last International Toy Fair in Nuremberg, toy mortars and such were reported to be not much in evidence.

I can live with war toys. I played with cap pistols on the streets of Baltimore when penny-candy cost a penny and, beyond a present inexplicable fondness for the gattling-gun sound of my typewriter, I came to no harm.

It's that super-mammal Barbie I can live without. I'd like to see the U.S.A. give her the Swedish slip. But I don't thing it will ever happen. At the annual American Toy Fair held in New York, Barbie was still the belle of the ball. She has been around for more than 30 years.

Barbie, who seems to be some kind of American Earth Mother, reproduces her remarkably proportioned self with an expensive variation every year. We have many Barbies. People give my daughter Barbies as casually as my grandfather used to give me shiny pennies.

Although we have many small trunks filled with Barbie clothes, our Barbies always seem to lounge about the house dishabille.

By dishabille, I mean that Bridal Barbie commonly wears only a veil; Superstar Barbie, naught but a handheld microphone; and Ballerina Barbie, just sunglasses as she stands locked in a plie before an audience of plastic soldiers and a ceramic Charlie Brown figurine.

"Let's get some clothes on all these Barbies!" I cry from time to time.

"Why?" ask the kids.

Yes, my innocence is long gone.

"Why?" they ask again and stare at me until I feel like an old-time missionary stepping out of a canoe with a handful of brassieres.

My wife says that I do more chores for Barbie than I do for her. It is true. Barbie has a tough life.

As my own household falls apart, I spend my time repairing Barbie's Corvette, replacing the string on her elevator and removing her motorcycle helmet from her head with pliers.

The other night, just as I was finishing replacing a Barbie head on a Barbie body, a child's voice from an upstair's bedroom called, "Quick! My piggybank fell off the shelf and smashed through the roof of the Barbie Townhouse. Help-murder-police!"

"Barbie got it good this time," I said that night as I rolled away a brass pig full of pennies and yanked her out from under the debris from the toppled Barbie Refrigerator. She was covered with little Barbie TV Dinners. Marie Osmond, who was sleeping nude on a sofa under a Kleenex, was unharmed.

Like ol' Brer Rabbit, Ken --the official Barbie consort-- sat in the Ken Van wearing one shoe, a canteen and a grin. As long as Mattel never makes him marry Barbie, he can sit in his van, drink canteen water with GI-Joe and smile at fools like me.

Barbie's legions will grow. There is now a Black Barbie and a Hispanic Barbie. No one is safe. And again they found a way to market yet another Caucasian Barbie. This year she provides an answer to that timeless trivia question: Who has longer hair than Crystal Gayle?

When Barbie first appeared in 1958, she was the first of her kind in our culture. But because she bears such a great resemblance to those female fertility figures whose history is traceable from some 400 centuries to the Aurignacian period, one wonders if Barbie is 31 years old or 40,031. It takes a long time for some things to come full circle.

I do not mean to make a blue joke of Barbie. After all, with six Barbies living under my roof, the joke is obviously on me.

My little daughter likes Barbie. But she also likes a very large and very old Raggedy Ann that has been passed down in the family.

Raggedy Ann is not anatomically correct --neither is Barbie for that matter-- but underneath her white apron and calico dress, there is stamped on her flat cotton bosom a little red heart. It is stamped on all authentic Raggedy Ann dolls. It says "I Love You" inside the heart.

I will not make a parallel observation about Barbie.

# ON THE BARREL HEAD

*Surviving the sword-in-the-heart stage of what seemed to be the operatically protracted death of the plastic standard in 1980 was not easy:*

Many small businesses can no longer afford to accept credit cards, and many consumers have had their credit limits reduced to unspendably small amounts, or have been discouraged from charging things because of increases in interest rates. Some folks have simply had their credit cards taken away, and new applicants are being turned down.

As a friend of mine once said as he stepped into the afternoon sun and winced after a three-martini lunch, "O brave new world."

At a little old-fashioned hardware store I usually frequent on Saturday mornings, there was quite a commotion the other day because of all the credit chaos. People don't seem to be taking well to using cold cash instead of a slip of plastic to buy things.

I was bent over a drawer of mixed bolts when I heard a woman's voice cry, "Filthy lucre!" A hush fell over the little store.

An elderly woman who looked like she was dressed for a formal brunch was at the cash register. She had a large rat trap in one white-gloved hand and a pack of spring-clip clothespins in the other.

"What do you mean by *money*?" she said indignantly.

"If you want this stuff, you have to give me *money*," the man at the cash register said.

The lady put down the rat trap and clothespins and with a stiff-wristed motion threw a credit card at the man. It flew at him like a little Frisbee and bounced off his shirt. He bent and picked it up and dropped the card in front of her.

"These things aren't any good here any more," he said. "I can't afford it. It's all over. You have to give me money."

"That's outrageous," she said. "I wouldn't think of doing such a thing."

The woman attempted to intimidate the man. She fixed unblinking eyes on him and pressed her lips together until they were white. She drew great heaving breaths through her nose. I could tell that her ploy was not working. She drew one last breath that shook her entire body and stalked out leaving the rat trap and clothespins behind.

"Next!" the man said.

A young couple presented themselves to the counterman. They had between them a can of spray paint, a garden-hose nozzle, a meat thermometer and a few packets of seeds. The counterman hit the "total" button and the young fellow held out a credit card.

"What's that!" challenged the counterman, apparently drunk on the blood of the dragon he had just slain.

"It's our ticket to the good life," the young wife innocently piped up. "Only 16 dollars separates us from ruin, but with this credit card we have the secure feeling that ruin is several hundred dollars away."

"Yes," her young husband interrupted, "instead of my wife and I feeling like we are only worth 16 dollars until I get paid next Friday, we can spend the week feeling like a few hundred bucks."

"Well in this hardware store, you two are only worth 16 dollars. But you're lucky--your bill comes to $15.98. That means you and your wife can leave here feeling like two cents."

Most of the people in the store had taken an interest by now in what was going on around the cash register. There was a buzzing sound like you used to hear in the movies when the film broke.

The young couple put the nozzle, paint and meat thermometer on top of the rat trap and clothespins. They bought the seeds. I guess they were trying to save a little face.

I counted the bolts in my hand and put two back in the drawer. When I stepped up to the cash register, I noticed for the first time that the old counter was gone and a that large barrel had taken its place.

"What gives?" I asked as I pointed at the barrel.

"Its simple," the man said as he counted the bolts. He looked up at me. The odor of dragon blood was thick. "You see this barrel head?" He thumped the top of the barrel. "You put your cash on it."

A neighbor was coming down the street as I left the hardware store. "How are you feeling today?" he asked.

I started to count the change in my hand.

# IT ALL DEPENDS

Do you know that number guitarist Pete Seeger plays called "Living in the Country"? There are no words. He plays it on his 12-string and whistles.

I live a few gallons of gas north of Baltimore in Harford, a cow-and-corn county that just doesn't seem like the country anymore.

It was country enough long ago when the Army thought it a fittingly forsaken spot for a proving ground and an arsenal. As cows mooed and corn winds blew, the Army tested tanks, howitzers, rockets, LSD and war chemicals.

The county has grown but the Army is still blowing up stuff and knocking plates out of china closets miles away.

On weekends, young soldiers, skin heads, crowd the fast-food restaurants in Aberdeen. They talk about Iowa, Alabama and about how much beer they are going to drink before they have to be back on the base. They place if-mom-ever-knew orders for dinner like "a shake and four packs of fries."

In the darkness outside, the town police get ready for a weekend of coping with a new problem for Harford County: prostitutes, many of whom drive up from Baltimore for the weekends to visit Uncle Sam and his merry men.

When I moved to Harford County you could buy a house there for about $10,000 less than you could buy the same kind of house around Baltimore. But housing is no longer the bargain it once was ever since Harford County caught on as a suburb of the suburbs of Baltimore. If the northern migratory trend continues, my little children will probably buy their first houses in Philadelphia, get home delivery of *The Sun* and root for the Orioles.

So many people have moved from Baltimore and its suburbs to get away from it all, that "it all" has re-emerged in Harford County.

Not long ago, my development of aluminum-sided houses --which sits cheekily in the middle of a corn field-- received word that a shopping center was going to be built in the adjoining fields. Some of the neighbors are fighting it. Others sort of sense it is something inevitable, something we brought on ourselves by coming into the corn in such great numbers.

The roads outside of Bel Air used to be almost empty. I could drive the main road from my development to the on-ramp at Interstate-95, which I use to get to work, in a flash. You didn't have to worry too much about putting a quarter in the unmanned toll machine. That was a while ago.

Now the road that passes my development resembles York Road at rush hour. The cars are often backed up a half-mile at the toll machine. And, from time to time, a State policeman squats behind the toll machine with a radio and calls ahead to his buddies down and around the bend in the ramp when you stiff the machine.

The last time they did this, 17 cars were pulled over as I drove by. Harford County has lost its innocence.

A look at one of the back issues of the local weekly newspaper piled on my desk provides other indications that Harford County has come of age. Front-page items include news of the county executive pleading *nolo contendere* and being put on probation for failing to report a campaign contribution of $500, and the usual update on the activities of the Aberdeen prostitutes.

The late Jerry Turner, the Walter Cronkite of Baltimore's TV-news anchormen, made page two by speaking at a Harford fire-department banquet. The picture of Old Familiar at a podium appears next to the photo of a woman from Joppa posing with her pet dogs. She did the county proud by appearing as the centerfold girl in a national skin magazine.

Other pages recorded that the little grocery store just down the main road from me was held up by a guy with a shotgun and that the ice cream store where we take our kids was also robbed. On the back page was a picture of a door with "KKK" painted on it. It was the front door of the YWCA building at the entrance to my development. My daughter attends Brownie meetings there.

Some people talk about moving farther into the country. But I won't be moving: "It all" will only follow, if it isn't something we actually carry with us.

When I think of the cows that still graze in a postage-stamp pasture next to the parking lot at Harford Mall in Bel Air, I can whistle a little like Pete, about living in the country. On the cows, so much depends.

*Eight years after this piece was written, the owner of the pasture died, and the cows and land were sold for a shopping mall.*

# ONLY THE BEGINNING

"Many's the long night I've dreamed of cheese --toasted, mostly," said ragged Ben Gunn who had been marooned on Treasure Island for three years.

Luckier than Ben Gunn, I got a piece of the free cheese the government had been giving away to the poor in March of 1982. I am not a poor person, but I got a piece of the cheese anyway. Government plans tend to work like that.

I didn't get much of the cheese. I got just enough to cover a few crackers. But it was enough to prove that the channels are open and that a trickle-down economic system can work. Ever since Ronald Reagan became president, I had been waiting to get trickled on.

I got my taste of poor-people cheese from someone who is not poor either. He got it from someone who got it from someone and the block got smaller and smaller as it trickled along.

I didn't pay much attention to the chronicle of the cheese that lay on a sheet of foil on a table in the room where I eat lunch most days. I had the feeling that, in the argot of the street, the cheese might be hot. Perhaps, I thought, the less I know about this cheese, the better.

I decided to assume for the sake of my conscience that the cheese had crossed the hands of a *bona fide* poor person at one time, maybe someone who didn't like cheese and who was willing to pass and to wait patiently for the government to start trickling down something else to eat.

I know that I myself am waiting for the government to start trickling down Volvos, so it seemed a sufficiently seaworthy rationalization to weather a small moral storm.

It also occurred to me that I had not actively sought a hunk of the poor people's cheese; it had come to me. Someone in Washington had pushed the first valve down; the cheese had trickled down and around yo-de-ho-ho--ho-ho and it had come out here. There was no way to send the cheese back.

"This cheese is supposed to be for poor people," I said to everyone.

"You paid for it," someone said. "Eat it."

Although it is a fairly common belief, I have never thought that there is any connection between paying for something and deserving something. But I ate the cheese. The idea was too big for the moment. And I was curious to see what poor-people cheese was like.

The supplier of the cheese said that his wife had attempted to melt some of the cheese on top of a casserole the night before, but it would not melt.

"What happened to it?" someone asked.

"It just sat there," he said.

It seemed to me to be a cruel trick on the part of a smiling government to issue defective cheese to the poor. But, on second thought, there had been no outcry from cheese recipients that their cheese wouldn't melt. So I didn't make much of the complaint and thought that it might have been a punishment sent to my colleague for eating the poor people's cheese.

When others heard that the cheese would not melt on the top of a casserole, suspicions arose about the contents of the cheese.

Some began to worry that the cheese contained a mysterious ingredient and that the nation's poor were unknowingly being made a part of a great chemical experiment. Others thought that the cheese might contain an agent that an infrared camera could detect and satellites were taking pictures to see how the trickle-down flow pattern was shaping up.

I think the cheese didn't melt on the casserole because it was getting dry. The cheese was crumblier than what you expect of American cheese. It had the color and texture of English Cheshire and a taste that leaned on the palate's memory from American to Cheddar.

It was good cheese and I took a piece of it wrapped in a scrap of foil home in my briefcase.

I made the mistake of saying, "Wait til you see what I have for you," so my wife was not particularly impressed with the piece of cheese as I unwrapped it. It was about the size of a square on a checker board. And some heavy books had squashed it a little.

I told her about the casserole and the spy satellites as I looked in the refrigerator for the bottle of a pink California wine. This piece of cheese, a fated portion whether I deserved it or not, was going to go down in style. When the government stands you to a piece of cheese, you don't say no. I broke the cheese ceremoniously.

"To the president," I said with an upraised glass.

The Volvos can't be far behind.

# PLAYING THE GAME

Few people know what happened to all the Hula-Hoops we once had. I know.

Their sides were kicked in to form pie-slice smiles. Then they were shrunk and returned to us at a higher price as Pac-Men.

Whether or not to get a computer game to plug into the TV like everyone else has been a big issue around the house.

When the voice on TV asks, "Have you played Atari today?" the three kids always shout back, "NO!" from whatever corner of the house they are in. It's all my fault because I am no fun at all.

I have been against buying a TV-computer game on the grounds that anything that sweeps the country off its feet is usually nonsense. (It's true that I'm no fun at all.)

My wife sides with the kids and a recent assault on my wiser-than-thou position was mighty:

Didn't I go to Harborplace, for instance? Didn't I pay a lot of money there for a cup of barbecued chicken wings like everyone else even though I throw the wings away at home?

Didn't I go and get a free Smurf glass at the hamburger place like everyone else even though you had to pay 99 cents for the soda inside the free glass?

Didn't I have a shirt with a little alligator on it like everyone else? (It was a gift. I swear it was a gift.)

"And how much money have you thrown at the feet of Linda Ronstadt?" came the final roaring shot. Smoke filled the kitchen. I hadn't thought that buying all of Linda Ronstadt's records was throwing money at her feet, but I guess it is.

It was a humbling experience. The no-nonsense individualist, the Camel Man of the magazine ads that I fancied myself, had been torn to shreds. I never felt so much like Everyone Else in my life.

I have never been fond of Everyone Else. Everyone Else is always spending money.

He rents roto-tillers in the spring so his family won't have to turn the garden by hand. He builds sheds in his yard so his wife won't have to carry the kids' bikes up and down the basement stairs. He spends half his life at

Disney World. I know all this because my family is always telling me what Everyone Else is doing.

"But it still doesn't make much sense to buy a home computer game when everyone else has one. Let the kids play with theirs," I said to my wife.

"That's embarrassing!" the kids said.

Maybe it is. I know the oldest boy runs out in the morning and begins ringing doorbells until he gets invited in to play Pac-Man.

When I was a kid, I was out in the sunshine with my friends looking for soda bottles at construction sites. We would fill the baskets on our bikes with muddy bottles and then cash them in for the two-cent deposit. Then we would buy baseball cards and get nickel cokes from the machine with the handle you had to crank at the gas station.

Sometimes we would chip in our bottle money and split a pack of cigarettes. We would slip into the woods behind the gas station where there were milk cases to sit on and rain-stiff fragments of girlie magazines scattered around to look at.

Hmm. Maybe I should buy one of those computer games for the kids after all.

I have only played Pac-Man twice. I put a quarter token into a machine at an electronic-game arcade in Fallston but I didn't know how to work it and my game of Pac-Man was over so quickly that I slipped out of the place feeling like a jerk.

I tried it again at a bar on Belair Road in Fullerton only because someone in the group popped a quarter into the Pac-Man machine and turned to me and said, "Now it's your turn."

People gathered around to watch. I moved the yellow control knob randomly. I hoped that I might be accidentally doing something right. At first, the circle of people thought it was a clever new strategy I was employing. Then they started saying, "Hey! You don't know what you're doing!"

Maybe I don't know what I'm doing in being stubborn about buying the kids a computer game. In a few years, it is said, people who don't know anything about computers and working computer controls will be illiterates. And there is a school district in Orange County, California, that requires all graduates to complete a computer literacy course.

I did break down the other night and say that the kids could get a computer game. But not until Santa Claus comes. I don't want to get burned if the computer age goes the way of the Hula-Hoop by Christmas.

I'm just no fun at all.

# ONCE OVER LIGHTLY

Dingby said that suckers are born today at a greater rate than in P.T. Barnum's day. He was reading the label on my can of light beer.

"Light beer costs more than regular beer because it contains more water," Dingby said.

"That doesn't make sense," I said.

"That's right," he said.

A moose of a man swung through the door and moosed his way through the crowd to the bar.

"Watch this guy," said Dingby. "He'll just grunt, 'Beer.' "

"Gimme one of them low-calorie preppy beers," the moose said.

Dingby groaned. "What's this world coming to! That kind of guy used to be my favorite kind of guy." He dropped his head onto the bar.

Then Dingby told me about the origin of light beer as he came back to life and relit the tip of his cold cigar.

"It was in the back room at a yeast-haulers convention," Dingby said. He blew out his match. "All the big brewers are there and one of them says, 'How can we save money, boys?' And this other brewer cracks a joke and says, 'Let's water it down.' Everybody laughs, but then they start thinking that maybe an old idea is the best kind of new idea you can have anyway. 'The people will scream,' this one brewer says, but then another guy says 'you can trick the people by actually telling them that you're doing it and then charging them even more than what they pay for regular beer so they think they are getting something special.' "

It was the most outrageous story I had ever heard.

"I bet I can make light beer right before your eyes," Dingby said.

Dingby is fond of bar bets. He had learned about bar bets from his father who never worked a day in his life and supported a large brood of Dingbys for 37 years by betting people in saloons that he could stop the large electric fan, usually found running in the corner of a saloon in the old days, with his nose --which he could do.

I have met the elder Dingby who is now quite old and retired, and I believe the story because the old man is filthy rich even though he cannot read a word or recite a single multiplication table, and his nose is still intact.

Dingby is not quite his father's son and his favorite bar bet is to challenge someone to write the names of the twelve apostles around the edge of a bar coaster in five minutes. Dingby has made a lot of money --but nothing like the fortune his father amassed by sticking his nose into fans-- on his twelve-apostles bet.

"This is how you make light beer," Dingby said. He leaned over the bar and held his glass of draft beer that was one-third empty under the soda water tap. He pulled the tap and fizzed his glass to the rim. "That's how you make light beer," Dingby said. "And I'll bet you five you like it."

He handed the glass to me and I tasted it. He was right! It was a triumph for Dingby. It was better than the twelve-apostles bet. It was the finest light beer I had ever tasted.

"Gimme the glass," Dingby said. He passed the glass to the girl who was sitting on the other side of him. She was wearing a red dress with a slit in the skirt that ran to the waist. She looked 25 if not older, but she was actually a 17-year-old named Wendy who had been sent to the corner by her mother to buy a loaf of bread and had stopped off for a beer.

"Try this new kind of light beer," Dingby said.

The girl looked suspiciously at the glass. "How much does it cost?" she whined through her nose.

"This is not only cheaper than light beer, it's even cheaper than regular beer because of a special brewing process."

"I don't want to try it," she whined. "I only like things that cost more."

The remark had the effect of a tripped hammer on a bullet in an oiled chamber. Dingby flew into a rage. He delivered a torrent of loud observations about the size of Wendy's brain. He spoke passionately about light beer, light cheese, the meaning of life, the value of a dollar.

Then he looked about wildly and ran to the end of the bar.

"Hey, pal," he said to a guy. "Do you want a beer with half the calories and all the taste?" Before the guy could answer, Dingby drank half of the guy's beer and slammed the glass back onto the bar. He did the same thing to the next guy and the next guy. He worked his way around the whole bar. "Do you want a cheeseburger with half the calories?" he asked an old lady. He ripped her cheeseburger in half and stuffed one half into his mouth.

He tore around the place, eating and drinking and changing regular things into light things.

Then he began breaking chairs in such a way that each was left containing one-third fewer calories than a regular chair. "The truth will set you free!" Dingby screamed as he beat a chair against a wall.

At his trial, Dingby's lawyer told the judge the story of how Dingby's father had made his living by stopping electric fans with his nose, which the judge came to regard as a mitigating circumstance in the matter of Dingby's offenses. And an assortment of winos brought in by Dingby's lawyer impressed the judge with their knowledge of the twelve apostles. "I am going to give you a light sentence," the judge said to Dingby.

At the mention of "light," Dingby gave birth to a chuckle which evolved within two seconds into a hysterical laugh. The judge took this as a sign of disrespect and ordered Dingby to be executed.

Which actually happened.

Dingby had said that the truth will set you free. But I think it can kill you, unless you take things lightly.

# BLESS YE, BOXHOLDER

We may become a nation of silent streets and closed doors.

New goods and services are being marketed which increasingly allow us to live our lives without having to leave home.

Some areas have cable TV services which offer video catalog shopping.

Plastic pouches of frozen gourmet foods provide hotel-class meals without all the fuss of going out.

Home computers permit some people to do their office work at home and send it in on the phone lines.

With cable TV and a video cassette recorder, you can see all the movies you want without having to pay a babysitter or eat stale popcorn.

And many people are buying home exercise equipment and joining neighborhood tanning clubs so they can feel and look healthy without ever having seen the light of day.

We have always thought of ourselves as a mobile society, but lately we seem to be interested in sedentary pursuits.

Will the time come when we can't be manipulated by the oil-producing countries because we are happy and self-contained at home and we don't need gasoline to go anywhere anymore?

The sedentary revolution also seems to be entering the realm of religion.

The two most popular forms of religious expression in America are going to church and playing bingo. And both seem to be evolving into something new under the influence of the current stay-at-home craze.

In Harford County where I live, it is anticipated that cable TV subscribers will soon have the opportunity to play TV bingo on the public-access cable channel.

Players will buy their bingo-card booklets at local supermarkets and similarly convenient places. The proceeds will go to a worthy cause.

This means that charitable people who like bingo will be spared the rigors of playing church-basement bingo.

Church-basement bingo is fun only if you like sitting in a cold basement under harsh lights on a winter weekend night.

All the urns of strong black coffee brewed by old church-basement ladies do little to mask the army-tent scent of mildew that permeates everything.

Church bingos usually rely on donated prizes like bags of sugar and cans of lard, but the prizes on Harford County's TV bingo will be cold cash. When you win, you are supposed to call the station and yell Bingo! into the telephone. Maybe they will play a soundtrack with some canned groans on TV when the first call comes in.

I imagine this will be an improvement over church-basement bingo. What I will miss, though, are the slices of homemade cake with so much icing that they stick to the paper napkins they were served on and make a big mess.

It is not only church bingo that may be affected by the sedentary revolution. I think the very idea of *going* to church is about to change.

I recently received a letter from the pastor of the Church by Mail, Inc., in Atlanta, Georgia.

"God has laid your address on my heart," the letter begins. "I just feel that somebody at this address needs prayer."

Truer words were never spoken. "How did this man know?" I thought to myself.

I was personally touched until I noticed that the letter was addressed to *Rural Route Boxholder*.

The Church by Mail is founded on the belief that the Bible promises the "power to get wealth." The letter asks me to send in for a free Prosperity Cross.

On the back of the letter is a drawing of the cross from which golden rays emanate. Flying forth from the golden rays are five automobiles, three houses, a microwave oven, a speedboat, a refrigerator, a freezer, a washer and dryer, a Boeing 747 and a TV set. Scattered about is a sprinkling of U.S. currency.

Like other Christians, I have always wanted a Boeing 747 and I am still toying with the idea of sending in the card to get my free Prosperity Cross.

I think the Church by Mail will catch on now that our society is becoming more and more inclined to stay at home.

I guess we will keep the 747s in our driveways, just for show.

# LONG TIME PASSING

You can only imagine what the Old Testament wrestling match between Jacob and the angel would have been like if it had been fought by the rules of television wrestling:

Wrestlers must be thrown from the ring several times, landing at least once on the broadcast table; the referee must be ignored; TV commentators should express shock at all violations of the rules of good sportsmanship; the referee should be beaten and kicked by the loser and his manager at the end of a match; folding chairs and branding irons should be used in the ring; post-match TV interviews should feature everything from pie throwing to whipping people to the floor with leather belts; the arena audience should express disapproval by chanting "Bulls__t!" and this should be broadcast uncensored during children's prime-time TV hours on Saturday morning.

And I am sure a biblical referee would have said nothing about the angel wearing illegal wings, though the commentators would have screamed, "How can they let this happen!"

The recent ascent to stardom and household-wordhood of Hulk Hogan, Brutus Beefcake, Wendi Richter and the whole theatrical production company known as the World Wrestling Federation is difficult to grasp.

It seems to be fed by the interest of a generation of youngsters whose flower-child parents married with a vow that their children would not play with toy guns, eat Minute Rice, or pollute their karma with middle-class values or brown shoes.

Now their kids wear camouflage suits, play guerrilla war, drink Diet Coke and spend hours watching wrestlers strangling opponents with chains and biting foreheads until blood (juice to school-age aficionados) is drawn.

I don't know what happened, but TV wrestling now is serious business.

In one instance, a New York judge had to order two teenage brothers to stop watching wrestling shows --with the threat of removing the TV from the house-- because they were injuring each other practicing body slams and choke holds. One of the brothers, according to a newspaper account, had even put a deadly sleeper hold on his mother as she was stir-frying vegetables. (The mother lived to stir again.)

And Hulk Hogan was selected Man of the Year by the Community Mayors of New York, an honor that had been given the year before to New York's John Cardinal O'Connor. Hulk got to be guest ringmaster at the mayor's annual circus for handicapped and special children.

I wouldn't have known of Hulk Hogan's honor had I not read of it in *WWF Magazine,* a publication designed to corner the market on children's allowance money and to legitimate a freak show that would have made P.T. Barnum drool.

The article on Hulk Hogan tried to establish a link between the respectability of the government of New York, the poignancy of unfortunate children, the morality of the Catholic Church and the sado-masochism of the *WWF.*

The issue also makes a case that TV wrestlers are real athletes with an article on Hillbilly Jim's kneecap which was dislodged, to great public dismay, by Luscious Johnny Valiant. The article was written by the orthopedic surgeon who treated him, and it concludes with a box in which the editor sort of swears up and down that the author is a real doctor who maintains that Hillybilly Jim is a role model for physical fitness and not an actor in one-strap overalls.

The magazine fails in another attempt at class-by-association with a photo of the British Bulldogs, a popular tag team, at a tea party. The illusion of gentility is belied by the kidney pie-and-porter appearance of the two chaps and the I-wonder-what-this-stuff-is look they are giving the elegantly set tea table.

Some adults find TV wrestling "camp" --a mediocrity so extreme that it is perversely fascinating to the sophisticated. But what about the young viewers? To them, camp is what you do with a tent and a box of marshmallows.

On Saturday morning, "Hulk Hogan's Rock 'n Wrestling" cartoon show competes with the Smurfs and Punky Brewster, and kids want the new WWF wrestling dolls, Hulk Hogan lunch boxes and Iron Sheik school folders.

Something has happened to an old spirit that once walked the country in sandals.

Where have all the flowers gone?

Probably to a toy store to buy a Big John Studd doll as a confirmation or bar mitzvah gift.

So don't think twice, it's all right.

# DRIVING THE WRONG WAY

After a few minutes, I would turn on the radio and lean back in the seat. I could feel the work world slip away as wheels turned on the highway and time unwound. And distance from the job grew. There was a time when I enjoyed my drive home on Interstate 95 from the Baltimore Beltway to Route 24, Emmorton Road, in Harford County.

When I would leave I-95 and turn onto Route 24 heading toward Bel Air, I knew I was back in the country. A long, empty country road would take me home. I would drive and look at fields and woods, and here and there I would get a view of the distant southwestern horizon and dramatic sunsets.

Driving away from the I-95 umbilical gave me a sense of severance, and I would always consider how good it was to live in a tranquil place distinctly different and miles removed from where I worked. But now, with the rapid development of the Route 24 corridor, all that has changed.

The area of the Route 24 interchange on I-95 has burgeoned into a commercial district featuring motels, gas stations and fast-food restaurants. I am sure that alligator farms, circus worlds and other attractions associated with I-95 interchanges from Maine to Florida will be coming soon.

I moved to Harford County to get away from it all, and now "it all" has spread north from Baltimore county. The construction of stick houses with thin skins of aluminum siding abounds, especially along Route 24.

Route 24 from the interchange to Bel Air is so congested that residents along the road often feel trapped in their developments. And I am one of them.

Frustrated drivers have developed several techniques, all thoroughly unsafe, for entering Route 24 from side roads.

Lately, a turn onto the road with the flow of traffic is best accomplished by not waiting for an opening, but driving on the shoulder until a merging speed and an open spot are reached. I call this the Shoulder Slider.

But most people find themselves needing to turn against the flow of traffic. (Against-the-flow people tend to resent the ease with which with-the-flow people do shoulder-sliders and escape in the morning.)

One method used when attempting to turn against traffic is to go the other way and make a U-turn at some convenient spot. I call this the Wrong-Way-is-the-Right-Way ploy.

Some drivers who have the patience to wait in line at the mouth of a development to turn against traffic have given up on waiting for suitable openings in both lanes when they finally get to the head of the line. Often when a narrow break occurs, they just throw their cars across both lanes onto the opposite shoulder and drive on the shoulder until they can merge. I call this is the Headlong Plunge.

A deadly variation, used at times when the near lane is clear and the coveted far lane is jammed, is to drive on the wrong side of the road until you can merge. This I call Gambler's Gambit.

Once on the road, you find that tailgating is a form of defensive driving.

If you leave a safe distance behind the car in front, at the mouth of the next development not just one car but as many as five or six --responding to what I call the Prison Break syndrome-- will run the stop sign and spill out to fill in the gap, sending you braking and sliding into the shoulder to avoid rear-ending the last car.

But often the last car in a Prison Break will do a Headlong Plunge and take to the shoulder to avoid being rear-ended, leaving you closing quickly with not much in the way of alternatives.

At present, work on the new Route 24 bypass seems to be proceeding at a rapid pace. And I am wondering if it will be called Emmorton Road when it is completed. The present Emmorton Road is actually an improvement over what is now called Old Emmorton Road, which still exists in a few unconnected vestigial snippets. Perhaps the new bypass will be called Emmorton Road, and the present road will become Old Emmorton Road, with the traces of Old Emmorton Road renamed the Road of Something Lost.

It is something to consider while waiting for the alligators.

# PIER REVIEW

The Susquehanna River at Havre de Grace was frozen. It was supposed to be a mild day during a long freeze, but the day never warmed. It was 40 degrees. But the wind was down and the sun was bright on the ice.

I found rocks near the small public fishing pier and threw them over the edge to crack the ice. Then I lay on my stomach on the pier and used the butt of my fishing rod to push away the fragments to make a fishing hole.

At some distance from the pier was an unfrozen spot where gulls were diving in the water for fish. It looked beyond casting range for my light equipment.

I cast toward the clear water where the birds were fishing but the sinker and hook fell short and slid silently on the ice in the distance. The gears in my reel were already frozen and stiff to crank as I retrieved.

People visit the pier in all seasons, though traffic is heavier during warmer weather. It is a spot to stop for people who are taking a drive, and that day a woman with two small girls walked toward the pier. The children noticed distressed fish (what appeared to me to be shad fingerlings) thrashing spasmodically on their sides under the ice. I had noticed these fish when I arrived and I was not sure what to make of their condition.

Later, another car pulled into the parking lot. A man carrying a beer bottle walked to the pier.

"Catchin' an'thin'? he drawled.

"No," I said

"Ca'fis' allus hungry," he said.

The man grunted and threw his empty beer bottle out to where he suspected the ice was paper thin and he might cast. But the green bottle broke on the ice and fragments of glass made only the tinkling sound of a breaking Christmas tree ornament.

Not long after the sun began to work its effect and the ice began to break near the shore and withdraw slowly out into the river.

Another car pulled into the lot. I was beginning to feel like a host. Leaving his family behind, a man wearing a necktie and a tweed overcoat hurried toward the pier with a fishing rod.

"On the way home from church," he said to me. "Just thought I'd check things out." He reached into his pocket and produced a single night crawler wrapped in waxed paper.

He pinched off a piece and rewrapped the rest. He darted here and there jigging the worm up and down. "Maybe crappies," he said. That was what I had been hoping. I told him that a few weeks before a man had caught two nice ones from the pier. Then his family began honking the car horn and he left. I decided to call it a day, too.

But before I left Havre de Grace, I drove several blocks up the waterfront to see the new micro-park on the river underneath the Amtrak railroad bridge.

Apparently having trouble entertaining its troll population, the city built a postage stamp-size park under the bridge at a cost of $207,000. It was supposed to cost $65,000. But that's how things go.

Nevertheless, the state --which picked up most of the tab-- got its money's worth: The park has a gravel boat landing, moorings for about six small boats and a shed with two picnic tables. A row of pine saplings will eventually screen from sight the storage tanks of an adjacent fuel oil company. It is not often you get a deal like that for $207,000.

I, myself, think that the city should have used the money to buy fishing boats. I figure that $207,000 would buy about 750 small aluminum fishing boats and 1,500 oars.

The boats could then be given to deserving trolls trapped under bridges and on bleak, unfishable bits of shore --but who know, like me, that the fish are out there, somewhere.

# EDITING WATSON

# THE RETURN OF SHERLOCK HOLMES

As lightning flashed white, the rain which swept horizontally past the window turned silver. Thunder followed like sky-born locomotives falling into the streets of London.

I drew the curtain and lit the lamp by the window.

"Curious, this wind," I muttered.

"Indeed," said Mr. Sherlock Holmes as the yellow light from the lamp flowed into the room. "Not once this evening has it 'sobbed like a child in the chimney.' Times are changing."

"Really?" I said.

"Why, Watson, old boy, it's 1980," said Holmes.

"How thoroughly anachronistic for us to be about," I remarked.

"True," said Holmes, "but no one cares. In fact, I believe we will be about quite a bit now that 50 years have passed since the death of our creator, Sir Arthur Conan Doyle. You see, Watson, the copyrights which have protected us this last half century have now expired."

"It will be good to have the game afoot and us on the chase again." I said.

"It could be, Watson. But I am afraid the quality of our lives will depend very much on the talents of our recreators. Since the passing of Dr. Doyle, fine writers such as John Gardner, John Dickson Carr, Nicholas Meyer, and Conan Doyle's very own son, Adrian, have done well by us. But with the copyrights dissolved, any hack with a pencil and a paper bag can dabble with us."

Until this moment, the great detective had been lying languidly upon the couch. He then arose, affixed a letter to the mantle with his knife, filled his pipe with shag from the Persian slipper, scraped on his violin, glued clippings into his scrapbook, rang for Mrs. Hudson, thought about Irene Adler, ate cold meat from the sideboard, killed a tarantula with his walking stick, and fired his revolver into the wall.

It was good to be back with Holmes and the familiar routines of life at 221B Baker Street. For months, I had wandered the labyrinthine streets and mews of London looking without success for my long-neglected medical practice. And it was not but a few days before this violent night that I, a veritable Ishmael, returned to the comfortable lodgings of my bachelorhood and the company of Sherlock Holmes who so warmly received me.

Holmes returned to the couch with the foul clay pipe that had gone dead hanging from his mouth. The somber strain his bow drew from the violin filled our chambers with a palpable melancholy as the storm screamed like a wounded beast without and thrashed itself in agonized explosions of rage against the walls of Baker Street.

"We lie vulnerable, Watson," he said as he paused to strike a match and light his pipe. "We can be pushed about by anyone who can write a line or half as much."

"But Holmes, although there have been abuses during the last 50 years, we have, by and large, lived well enough in the hands of those true men of letters who have attempted to retrieve the fallen pen of our dear Dr. Doyle."

"I pray, Watson, that the wish of Lady Bromet be honored."

"Lady Bromet?" I said. I could not place the name.

"Why, Watson, I do believe that time has graced your memory with a thick layer of dust. Lady Bromet is Dr. Doyle's daughter."

"Dear me! Of course!" I said. "What did she ask?"

"Her request was simple. She asked that we be treated properly and with style by those who would write of us. Her remarks were reported in the newspapers this July on the 50th anniversary of the passing of her father." Holmes sat suddenly upright. "Listen!" he said. "There are footsteps on the stairs."

I listened intently to the faint tread I heard between the blasts of thunder. "I believe we will find that our caller is a Bolivian chemist to judge by his step," I said.

"Ah, good old Watson. Always trying to play detective," said Holmes. "I believe, Watson, that we will find that our visitor is the advertising representative of an American brewery who wants us to appear in a television commercial for a low-calorie beer now that we are free for the taking."

"You mock me, Holmes! All that cannot be told from a footstep."

"You are quite right, Watson. He telephoned this afternoon while you were out. Now quickly, as you value your life, bolt the door and let us weather this night by having a look inside that dispatch box you had sent 'round from the bank today."

Holmes was referring to the dispatch box containing all the records, published and unpublished, of our adventures which is kept in a vault at Cox's Bank at Charing Cross.

"There is a detail or two," said Holmes, "of which you had no knowledge, that should be added to your account of that monstrous affair concerning the giant rat of Sumatra."

"It feels like old times," I said.

"Let us hope that all our times are old times, Watson," said Sherlock Holmes.

# THE ROYAL WEDDING OF SHERLOCK HOLMES

Old bachelors, as it is commonly known, become fixed in their ways. And I believe I may safely assert after an acquaintance of 100 years and some odd months, that there is no bachelor with more intractable habits than Mr. Sherlock Holmes.

It is for this reason that I was greatly surprised one morning in July of 1981 to find the renowned detective missing from his usual spot at the breakfast table by the opened bow window overlooking the ebb and flow of mankind on Baker Street. I tapped at the shell of the warm egg which had just been served by Mrs. Hudson and found myself disturbed as I stared at the unattended egg perched in its cup across from me at Holmes's place.

Though Sherlock Holmes is widely regarded as a timeless man, it had been for some time my opinion as a medical man that Holmes's many years were catching up with him. And, despite his many protests, I believed that his recent secret involvement in the matter of the exile of a Mid-Eastern political figure had taken its toll on his health.

With this thought, my moment's wonder gave way to alarm and I flew to the door of his chamber at once. When I threw open the door, I found that Sherlock Holmes was gone. I stood with the knob of the door in my hand. His bed was undisturbed, but an envelope addressed to me in his familiar hand lay upon it. Inside the envelope was the most extraordinary message I had ever received from Sherlock Holmes: "Watson--I have gone to take a bride. You may eat my egg if you wish. S.H."

"Take a bride! Why, Holmes, you are 127 years old!" I exclaimed as if he were standing before me.

But, upon saying this, my thoughts were instantly arrested by what seemed a riotous commotion in the hall downstairs. Mrs. Hudson was shrieking as if death had leapt through the door at her. I thrust the letter from Holmes into the pocket of my jacket, ran and drew my heaviest stick from the basket and darted out to the top of the stairs.

Then, as if I had been bludgeoned, I stopped with my stick upraised and beheld a sight which even in this moment of retrospect still makes my soul shake. There, in the sunlit hall below by the still opened door to 221 Baker Street, stood the Prince of Wales in the company of his intended bride, the most beautiful young woman ever to have risen to prominence in England.

"Your loyalty to Mr. Holmes is legend, Dr. Watson," he said, "but I'd no idea you carried it so far." He gazed briefly at the stick I still held over my head as he addressed me. "I assure you I seek only a brief word with Mr. Holmes," he continued.

"But," I gasped hoarsely and without any presence of mind, "Holmes is not here!"

"Then a word with you, Dr. Watson, will suffice." Which being said and without further ado, the royal couple ascended the stairs. As the young woman passed me and entered the humble bachelor's lodgings of myself and Sherlock Holmes, her head seemed to nod and she smiled upon me with upturned eyes.

The Prince of Wales strode briskly ahead of her into the room and with his hands clasped behind his back surveyed the room.

"What a dump!" he said as he looked about.

"I say!" I said.

"Why, your stories are true. You and Holmes are as messy as mice," he said as he wandered near the breakfast table. "Do you think it safe to keep a jar of strychnine by the sugar bowl?" he said as he tapped at a blue chemical jar which sat among the breakfast things. "And here," he said as he crossed to the cookie tin and raised the lid, "we find a revolver. Really, Dr. Watson!"

"I say!" I said again.

"But now, Dr. Watson, let's get right to business. I have come here today to ask you to pull my nose."

"I say!"

"It's that simple," the prince said as he approached me. I drew back a step and involuntarily spun around, whereupon I suddenly heard the unmistakable voice of Sherlock Holmes say, "If you won't pull the nose of the Prince of Wales, Watson, then I shall!" At the sound of Holmes's voice, I turned in shock to see the prince seize his own nose and tear it from his face. Then his fingers tore at pieces of rubber on his face until before me stood not the Prince of Wales, but Sherlock Holmes!

"You must pardon the deception, my good Watson, but I had to be certain of the effectiveness of the disguise.

"But--" I said as I looked toward the young woman.

"No, Watson, it is not Lady Diana at all. Allow me to introduce the famed actress and operatic star, Miss Irene Adler."

I fell back in my chair under the weight of it all. Ever since Holmes's encounter with Irene Adler in May of 1887, the famous encounter which I documented in a story called "A Scandal in Bohemia," she was always *the* woman to Sherlock Holmes. For the last 94 years, her portrait in evening dress, which Holmes had received from the King of Bohemia, enjoyed a prominent place among the clutter on his desk.

"But what is the meaning of all this, Holmes!" I finally managed to say.

"Elementary, Watson, In these troubled times, men and women of high place are not safe in the public view. For this reason, and in these very disguises, Miss Adler and myself will be married next week in St. Paul's Cathedral before the eyes of the world in the place of the real Prince and the future Princess of Wales."

"But what of the wedding of the real royal couple?"

"That has been arranged, Watson. The Prince of Wales and his charming bride, disguised as Americans, are in Reno, Nevada, where they will be married discreetly and in safety."

"Disguised as Americans?" I said.

"Yes," said Holmes. "The Prince of Wales is to wear a T-shirt with the picture of a can of beer on it and Lady Diana is to wear red terry shorts and a garment known as a tube top. Every detail has been carefully attended. I understand that they will even put chips in her toenail polish so that she really looks like an American woman."

"But what of you and Miss Adler?" I said as I thought of the note he had left which was still in my pocket. "Will not you two then be actually married at St. Paul's?"

"Of course not, Watson. The ceremony will be slightly faulted. I will omit one word from the wedding vow and Miss Adler in pronouncing her vow will address me as 'Philip Charles' instead of 'Charles Philip.' I am sure the world will note it only with amusement, but its true significance will never be suspected."

How the "royal couple" honeymooned was a matter of speculation in the press, but I hoped that Holmes was enjoying himself. While Holmes and Miss Adler were aboard the Britannia, a postal card arrived for Holmes from the Poconos Mountains in Pennsylvania. The picture on the card showed a man and a woman bathing together in a heart-shaped tub of soaps suds. The back of the card contained no message.

# DEDUCED RECKONING

# THE RIGHT DIRECTION

You had to douse all fires and be as quiet as a mouse when the president went to bed at Camp David --even if you were sleeping on the ground a mile away.

Sharing a mountain with Richard Nixon gave me a few tense moments, but it was still one of the best weekends of my life. It was the last time I saw the stars.

The other night, when I took the trash cans out to the curb, the moon was almost overhead. It was round and white. Perhaps because the sky was clear and the moon was so intensely bright, the moon did not appear disc-like, flat in the sky, as usual. It was surprisingly orbiculate. For a moment, I was stunned that it did not fall.

Beneath the moon, the short winter grass glowed almost green, like outfield turf under ballpark lights.

I arched my neck again and looked for the stars. I could not see the stars very well. The post-lights at the street ends of the driveways and the lights from the shopping center not far away turn the sky to milk every night.

There have been few occasions when I have been far enough from light to see all the stars. That night, as my trash cans sat gleaming under the post-light, I could only see a few of the brighter stars. I found myself in the curious position of cursing the light instead of the proverbial dark.

Many of my high school students have never seen the star fields spread cold and deep from horizon to horizon. The subject of stars surfaces every year around this time when the 11th graders read Walt Whitman's "When I Heard The Learn'd Astronomer." This eight-line poem is about a man who becomes weary for "unaccountable" reasons while attending a famous astronomer's lecture where mathematics, charts and abundant applause fill the room. The man slips away from the lecture hall and wanders off in the night, fully satisfied to look up from time to time "in perfect silence at the stars."

I tell my students about the stars. Some go out and look for them; others are content with having seen them in TV shows or movies about UFOs or rocketship heroes.

In either case, I cannot work up a condescending smile. I was not much younger than my students when a scoutmaster at Broad Creek showed me the stars for the first time; that night was so dark and clear that the scoutmaster used a flashlight's beam for a pointer. And now that I am much older, I can still sadly count on one hand the number of times I have clearly seen all the stars.

The last time I saw all the stars was from a slope in the Catoctin Mountains which was apparently within electronic earshot --if not actual earshot-- of Camp David. I was a chaperone on a high school camping expedition.

A first-term Nixon was at Camp David that weekend. The park ranger on duty at the gate eyed us suspiciously and admitted us to the park with great reluctance. He warned us to be absolutely silent after 10 p.m. The ranger made a big deal of our being quiet. As a result, the kids made a lot of noise, shouting rude things about the president until well after midnight.

I lay there that night, looking up at every star a man could ever hope to see at once, and all I could do was worry about waking up Richard Nixon.

I waited for dogs and Marines to come pouring out of the brush. But after everyone settled down, we began to lose ourselves in the stars. We talked for a long time, very quietly, about what we saw.

Looking at the stars alters perspective. Our galaxy, the Milky Way, is a spiral nebulae --an S-shaped pinwheel of over 300 billion stars. Near the middle of one of the blades, Earth revolves around one of the smaller stars that is our sun.

It is a chilling thought which gets downright icy when you realize that the Milky Way is but one of a billion galaxies of which we know among an estimated trillion. It is hard to believe that there are other galaxies, but from the Southern Hemisphere, two nearby galaxies called the Clouds of Magellan can actually be seen with the naked eye.

I do not know much about the stars. I confess that on the night I took the trash cans out to the curb, I smugly located the North Star in what I now realize to have been the eastern sky. But all you really need to know is how to look up, which is what Walt Whitman was saying.

It is a cruel irony that we are blinded by our own lights. We never have the chance to look up and see where we really are.

# OUT OF TIME AND SPACE

Black Dots on ceilings tend to come and go. It is a waste of time, as we all know, to try to figure them out. Most black dots are mysteries. But sometimes they are spiders.

Spiders seldom visit us other than at dinner time when we are preoccupied with feeding little children. That's why spiders always feel it's necessary, I think, to walk on the ceiling over the table to get our attention.

Everyone began to squeal the other night when a black dot appeared on the ceiling over the table. Chairs were pushed back at once. The reception was worthy of King Kong. "Get it!" I was charged, as if all I had to do were snap my fingers to bring to my side a bearer with a rifle full of high-velocity ceiling-dot shot.

I looked at the roast beef as it bubbled juice and at the unstained carving tools that lay beside it. I decided to bluff. "I don't think that's a spider," I said, "It's just a black dot."

"It's moving --get it before it falls in our milk!" everyone screamed. The bluff was done.

Even though black dots on ceilings over beds cause panic and domestic upheaval, spiders in our milk is the biggest thing we worry about.

"It's coming down! It's coming down now!" everyone cried.

"Give him a little time," I said. "He will be easier to catch if I wait for him to come to me."

Down the spider came. He was playing out his line. Not all at once, but little by little. The offspring of the god-defying peasant Arachne rappelled against the invisible walls of space.

Arachne was a proud mortal maiden who challenged the goddess Athena to a weaving contest. Before the eyes of equally haughty Athena, Arachne made a dazzling tapestry depicting the evils of the gods and was touched with wolfsbane by the outraged and outwoven goddess. Arachne withered and her fingers became affixed to her sides.

In place of threads of gold and Tyrian purple, she and her newly made kind would spin forever with threads the color of air. Olympus fathered irony, as well as spiders.

Perhaps our fear of spiders is inordinate. Children are taught to loathe spiders by well meaning parents who chant by moonlight the story of Miss Muffet until their babies grow to shiver at the thought of a spider, not to mention such other harmless things as tuffets --which are tufts of grass, not milking stools as many nursery-rhyme illustrators are fond of envisioning them. (Yes, I do concede that a healthy fear of curds and whey may be beneficial.)

The spider, not bigger with his legs extended than a pencil eraser, blew silk from the many jets in each of his six nipple-like spinnerets. The silk melted into one unseen thread. He came down a little closer to me. My hand reached out to test the distance. He curled. He quickly moved up an inch or two.

The mashed potatoes under him looked hard. The milk was getting warm. The roast beef was metamorphosing into a football.

The spider is about as old as the earth. He was among the first to crawl out of the primordial pea soup and take to land. Man, it is said, was not around at that time. Given the depth of the spider's collective unconscious, the size of this planet and its countless opportunities, I could not understand why a spider would come to my house to descend into a glass of milk.

Finally, I put a hand on the table, made a leap and grabbed the spider. I felt him tickling my palm. I had the choice of squishing him at once, flushing him down the drain at the kitchen sink or opening the back door and chucking him out into the yard.

Spiders are easy to catch because they don't see very well. Although they have eight eyes, they cannot see clearly beyond a few inches. Maybe that's why the spider was rappelling out of time and space into our supper. Man is like the spider, I suppose. Because he is larger, he can see mountains, horizons, stars. But he can't see much beyond that.

I lost the spider before I got to the back door. I didn't tell anyone. I don't know where he went. I just pretended and waved my empty hand into the night.

# THE BIG TWO-HEARTED PERCOLATOR

Although he never complained about Miss Kitty's beer, Matt Dillon seldom seemed to have a good word for Chester's jailhouse coffee. Hardly an episode of "Gunsmoke" was filmed in which the marshal of Dodge City didn't scowl at least once into his tin cup:

"Chester, how old is this coffee?"

"I just changed them grounds last week, Mr. Dillon."

Life was tough in the Old West. So was the coffee.

Ernest Hemingway once "hemingwayed," a verb of the moment, about making coffee. To "hemingway" is to speak of something ordinary, like making coffee, as if it were quite meaningful. Nick Adams, the sole character in "Big Two-Hearted River," seems to suffer a third-class dark night of the soul in the Michigan woods as he wonders whether he should make his campfire coffee his way or "according to Hopkins." Hopkins, his old fishing buddy, boiled the grounds.

The story also contains a lot of "hemingwaying" about Nick Adams eating his canned apricots and making an onion sandwich. The onion sandwich is my favorite part of the story. Some people think that reading about a man who doesn't do too much more in a story than fish for trout, eat apricots and make coffee is a lot of bologna. But Hemingway's fascination with the commonplace --with the smells, tastes, sights, in-hand feelings of life-- is about as close, I think, as Western man can climb to the spiritual heights of the East where smiles of wisdom can be provoked by the light of a firefly, the sound of water.

Making coffee can be important.

Nick, eventually, made his coffee "according to Hopkins" and the grounds boiled over into the fire. Life was tough in the Michigan woods.

Where I live and make coffee, life is tough, too. It's tough because I seldom have time to stop and brew coffee. I have to settle for a cup of the instant stuff which I drink in the car on the way to work. Just about everyone who drives the stretch of Interstate 95 I use every morning drinks coffee behind the wheel. It seems to have become a part of the fast-paced American way.

A visiting professor of French culture at Johns Hopkins University once said that what he found most remarkable about Americans is that they seem to live in their automobiles. He was a very small Frenchman who suffered from hay fever and who put very small French sniffles into oversized American man-handler tissues and discarded each tissue after each sniffle as if it had just been used to wipe up a nuclear spill.

"You Americans do all kinds of things in cars which the French would never do," he more or less said. "Today, I went driving and I saw a man (sniffle) eating a sandwich in his car. You wouldn't see that (sniffle) in France."

I defensively observed, not aloud, that the French really ripped through a lot of Kleenex.

Americans like speed and efficiency. This is why so many people drink instant coffee as they drive to work. Even when Americans have vacations, they refuse to leave their automobiles. They fill their cars with children, crackers, pillows, toys, maps, electronic games, thermos bottles and speed away. They drink coffee and eat hamburgers in their cars to save time.

What I have always done on my vacations is park the car, stay home and make real coffee. I do it very deliberately and intently--like Nick Adams. It's a pure and simple thing to do.

But, lately, I wonder if I am kidding myself. I find myself preparing my morning coffee the night before and plugging the percolator into a timer. Instead of enjoying the smell of a freshly opened can of coffee and touching the cool brown coffee grounds, I am preoccupied with the tangle of electric wires and getting the timer adjusted so that the coffee will be done brewing at the exact time the morning paper will be plopped onto the driveway. I do not really have the spiritual depth to sit around and smile wisely like an Eastern monk if I have to wait for my coffee.

It has crossed my mind that I may not be enjoying my vacations as much as I think. It might be better if I fill the car with half the house like everyone else, give scandal to France and speed off with a jar of instant coffee.

# A HANDLE ON THINGS

People run into the woods at the first nip of autumn to look at colored leaves, to taste mountain spring water before they dig in for their long winter's work. I am no exception.

It is thought that looking at colored leaves and drinking spring water at its source while wearing heavy shoes and a checkered flannel shirt will help you get a handle on things.

People hunt in the woods for handles the way children hunt for Easter eggs. Lucky people emerge from the mountains in Western Maryland, Pennsylvania or Virginia with handles. Many use them as paperweights on their desks at work.

The monks at the Trappist monastery in Berryville, Virginia, live all year in the country frequented by autumn tourists. It is a long time since I was there. It was autumn then and I guess I was looking for a handle.

When I was there, the monks kept cows, pigs, chickens, made butter, baked bread and worked in their fields.

The house for guests, an old farmhouse, was a half mile or so from the main buildings. It sat at the end of a dirt road on a small hill. The first monk I was to meet came speeding in an old wreck of a car toward the guesthouse. He threw the car into a tight turn and slid it to a stop in an explosion of dirt and dust. In his grasp as he leaped from the car was a rifle with a telescopic sight. He fired a round which cracked into the yellow stubble of a harvested field.

He said he had fired at a groundhog and he was pleased that he had killed it. He was wearing dungarees and a Navy watchcap. He apologized for all the dust he had kicked up when he stopped the car. He said that the car had no brakes whatsoever and that was how the monks had to stop it. He said that visitors were bound by no rules and left.

For the next few days, pails of raw milk, loaves of bread, bowls of beets would be found on the steps of the guesthouse. When they are not firing guns and driving cars like Clint Eastwood's Dirty Harry, monks slip around very quietly.

Because I had felt a bit awkward asking about the meaning of life of a man dressed like a derelict and armed with a rifle with a telescopic sight, I fell to my own devices.

The old farmhouse was filled with flies, both living and dead. There were inches of flies in the light fixtures overhead, inches of dead flies on the window sills; there were even dead flies in the desk drawers. I was sure that if I were to find a handle on things, it would be under a foot of dead flies. In the beginning, I would take a spoon at the table and fish for my beets very carefully so that I wouldn't draw up the dead flies floating in the bowl. By the time I left, I learned to think nothing of having dead flies mixed with the beets on my plate.

It is such a change in attitude which indicates, I think, that your fingertips may be just starting to come near the handle on things.

The monks arise every three hours during the night to pray. I set the alarm clock and walked to their chapel a few times. One night, under the needlepoints of stars, I encountered a monk who was bringing cows down from a hillside near the guesthouse. I recall walking toward him and very profanely lighting a Marlboro with a Zippo as I drew near. I called good morning to him. He had been yelling at the cows but he would not speak to me. He smiled at me and bobbed his head as he passed. The metal clasps on his wide, unbuckled boots jingled. He was banging a cow on the rump with a flashlight to get it into the milking barn.

I felt like a jerk for barging into his silent world. I am sure he thought, "Next year, why don't you go to Luray Caverns."

It has taken me many years to realize that the flashlight in the monk's hand was really a handle. Not everyone who holds a flashlight has a handle on things. It all depends, I think, on your ability --or possibly your humility-- to accept a flashlight, a hammer, a pencil as a handle.

The leaves are starting to turn again. It is the season of soft decay. I will load the family into the car and we will drive into the country like so many others.

# I TO I

In the clock-tick quiet before dawn one morning, I popped on the light in the bathroom, looked into the mirror and found that I was not there.

It's finally happened, I thought.

It was a marvel. It is the kind of thing that happens to other people; you never think it will happen to you.

Actually, the mirror over the sink was not there. I had removed it when hanging wallpaper the day before. My fingers reached exploringly toward the unfamiliar, eye-stopping field of plaid vinyl.

The sensation that I had ceased to exist lasted just a moment, but a bathroom without a mirror is still a kind of Sartrian hell.

Forgetting to put a protective thumb over the sideburns when working in that area, I shaved by feeling my face. I guessed at where the part in my hair should be. All day long I had explain my appearance to people. I looked a little like a punk-rock star.

But what I missed most that morning was the daily chat most of us have with ourselves while looking in the bathroom mirror. The mirror over the bathroom sink is a Socratic niche. It invites daily discourse, philosophic dialogue between self and self.

Mirrors are not like pictures or paintings. We look *at* pictures of Ronald Reagan or of Meryl Streep in a magazine, for instance; we look *at* a painting of a great battle which covers an entire wall in a national museum. But we look into the mirrors. No matter how small, we look into them as if they were wells.

The most well-known case, perhaps, of someone who was lured too close and went right through a mirror was Lewis Carroll's curious Alice. She climbed to the mantle over the fireplace and slipped through the looking-glass.

Mirrors give a sense of depth. The bathroom mirror permits us to look at ourselves as through a window.

The optical trick of a mirror is a cleaving magic for we are separated illusorily from ourselves whenever we look into one.

The sensation of real separation occurs because the human eye, when it looks into a mirror, does not focus on the reflective surface as it does when looking at a photograph of Miss November or a painting of George Washington.

Instead, the eye focuses somewhere behind the mirror at a distance equal to the amount of space between the real object and the front of the mirror.

We take the separation of self from self when looking into a mirror with a degree of nonchalance today. But this was not always the case.

Some primitive cultures believed that the mirror image was actually the soul. They felt that the soul was mortally vulnerable when detached from the body. They avoided letting their image, their soul, lie on the surface of a stillpool lest a water beast eat it or an evil god living in the pool snatch it away. Some contemporary primitives still believe in a like way that the camera steals the soul and they will not allow themselves to be photographed.

But among the more advanced cultures today, primitive beliefs associated with mirrors still abound.

Dentists usually begin their treatment by sending a mirror on the end of a wand into a patient's mouth. It seems an attempt at making a quick buck by stealing away the patient's cavities with a mirror. Young men wear mirror sunglasses on the beach in an attempt to steal the souls of pretty girls. Some people even put mirrors over their beds to confuse evil spirits which may come in the night.

Mirrors fascinate us. Who can pass a three-way mirror in a clothing store without stopping to see if you can see the back of your head if you look and turn just the right way?

At a reception I once attended in a mirrored hall, I noticed how preoccupied many guests were with viewing things by looking into the mirrored walls. Some thought you could see things better that way, that the party had a more glamorous and dramatic sweep. It really was somewhat like watching a czar's ball in a film epic being shown on a wide screen.

Others were disconcerted by the mirrors. "They make me nervous," I overheard one person say. I think the mirrored room bothered some because it is disorienting to see yourself as part of a scene when we ordinarily spend most of our lives seeing little more of ourselves than our hands, shirtfronts and shoes.

My mirror is back in place now and very firmly screwed on the wall. It is not impossible, I have always thought, for the wind to blow through a mirror.

# DREAMING OF EARTH

There was a time when keeping your feet off the ground was the thing to do. Montezuma and the mikados of old Japan --just two examples-- were carried by their subjects when they went about and when they were at the palace they always kept a tapestry or a mat between their feet and the ground. They did this so they wouldn't discharge their powers into the earth. It was a somewhat electrical notion about human potential of which vestiges remain. Red carpets are still rolled out to safeguard the really supercharged among us and brides are careful to walk to the altar on insulating runners so they won't short-circuit their blushing glows.

But most of us today place a high value on keeping a foot on the ground.

Huck Finn, an archetypical real-American, always was happiest when the Mississippi mud was running between his toes. Then Widow Douglas, whom Huck described as "dismal regular and decent," took him in to "sivilize" him. She gave him good clothes, schooling and --in the tradition of Montezuma and the mikadoes-- a scrap of carpet for his room.

But he often stood at night by the window and looked to the woods and stars.

The ancient fathers of Greek civilization sent us a warning in a story thousands of years ago about the dangers of civilization. They knew that idea would catch on, I think, and that it would eventually get out of hand. Antaeus, a giant wrestler in this forethoughtful Greek legend, drew his strength from the earth. Whenever he was thrown to the ground, he surprised his opponent by springing back with renewed vigor. But Antaeus, who was roofing his house with skulls of those he defeated, was brought to ruin by Hercules. Hercules held the earth-fed giant in the air until his power dissipated. It was a good trick. Hercules then easily strangled Antaeus aloft.

I think the Greeks were trying to put a flea in our ear, as the old saying goes.

Americans who spend their days in office buildings of Herculean height often feel a mysterious draining and tugging at their innermost parts as they are taken aloft by elevators each morning. Sharpening pencils, handling papers, breathing recirculated air, they spend time under cold blue-white lights, weakening, waiting. They often stand and, dreaming of earth, look from their windows with Huckleberry eyes.

"We'd never make it," he says as he gauges the drop.

"The windows don't open anyway," she says. "They knew what they were doing when they built this place."

They go back to work.

Even if windows in the new office building did open, it's still hard to grow a leg long enough to keep a foot on the ground from the umpteenth floor.

Some days when I am driving to my building with a necktie at my throat and a briefcase full of papers on the seat beside me, I start wondering how the guys with the big tool boxes in the mud-splashed pickups cruising down the highway with me are going to spend their day. The pick-up truck guys usually have whiskers and they look like they are wearing comfortable old clothes. Their dashboards are littered with little pie boxes and tape measures. They don't have to worry if they slosh some convenience-store coffee on their pants while they are driving to work. Maybe where they are going there will be a barrel with lumber scraps burning in it. Maybe at lunch they will sit by the flaming barrel on low benches made from concrete blocks and boards.

They can smell smoke and look at the sky.

In 1841, in the days before he wrote *The Scarlet Letter*, Nathaniel Hawthorne joined the Brook Farm commune where the high thinkers and Transcendentalists of Boston in a classic experiment donned work clothes and tried their hands at farming and common labors. In the beginning, Hawthorne dutifully shoveled at the dung heaps assigned to him and joyously appended "Ploughman" to his signature on a letter to his sister. But he came to find that he was always too tired to think or write at day's end. Within a few months, he thought of his tenure on the farm as "bondage," and he bitterly wrote to his fiance, "Labor is the curse of the world."

White-collar workers often have blue-collar dreams. And maybe their dreams really are just that. Some of the guys I often envy in the trucks with earth-clogged tires don't get paid if it rains and they can't work. A guy like that has to come home with his lunchbox unopened. His wife, as often happens, spends the rest of the day slamming an iron around on an ironing board and asking him why he doesn't get another kind of job, something "dismal regular and decent," perhaps.

But most days, it seems to me, it doesn't rain.

# PROMISES, PROMISES

The bright, compact, gold and silver ingot-like cans always seem to promise something more than a double row of headless and tailless fish.

For that reason, I buy a can of sardines every year or so. It takes about that long for me to forget that I don't like sardines. Most cans of sardines are sold to people like me. I am told that I always say, "I guess I forgot what they look like," after I open my annual can. There are worse fates, but I know that I am doomed to saying that once a year for the rest of my life.

Canned sardines don't have heads because, I think, they die laughing. Sardine purveyors remove the heads so their trade will not be ruined by the smiling fish who are in on the scam. Their tails are also removed so sardines can't be flipped like coins and put to some useful purpose after people open the cans and see how they look.

Life is full of sardine-type tricks and even little children pay the price.

Kids think that kites really can fly, for instance. Every spring, little kids can be seen running for blocks dragging kites behind them. The kites usually thrash colorfully, wildly against sidewalks and parked cars until their wooden bones are broken.

Once, though, on the windy beach at Ocean City, my own kids did manage to send a kite far out over the ocean at the end of what had to be three dollars worth of overpriced boardwalk string. But, life being what it is, after everyone got a turn at holding the string, the kite, a dot in the dull evening sky, took a nosedive and plunged like a brick into the ocean.

I believe that the kite was lured to its death by a passing school of sardines. Kites and sardines have an occult affinity in that they both bring more disappointment to life than joy.

Many people on the beach were sympathetic about the kite and the three-dollars' worth of boardwalk string. I said that when you come right down to it, it is easier to fly a sardine than a kite. The youngsters in collegiate sweatshirts thought that sounded pretty funny, but old, wizened heads nodded knowingly about sardines, kites, the cruel void between expectation and reality, and the miseries of life in general.

One of the most long-lived sardine-type tricks is the notion that you can make a fire by rubbing two sticks together.

The driving force behind this myth is the Boy Scouts. My ever-handy 1956 edition of their handbook suggests rubbing sticks together to start a fire "in an emergency." Whenever there is an emergency, according to the handbook, all you have to do is whip out some tinder, charred cloth and two pieces of the recommended quaking aspen or Arizona yucca.

Even Jack London in his classic story of Yukon survival, "To Build a Fire," did not strain credulity by having his hapless hero stave off death with two sticks of Arizona yucca. London placed 70 sulphur matches between the freezing man and death. Given 70 matches and 70 chances, the man still could not make a fire and he froze to death.

A while back during the winter snows, little children were in our yard rubbing two icy sticks together. I raised the kitchen window and squinted out toward them. The sun was setting whitely and blindingly behind a stand of bare cigar-brown trees. It was like looking into the beam from a cop's flashlight and the earth seemed hard.

The kids said they were trying to make a fire and they asked me why it wasn't working. They were standing in a circle taking turns rubbing the sticks together. Each kid rubbed the sticks more furiously than the one before.

"Why is it that everything people tell you isn't true?" my oldest son who was among the group asked. Eventually, they threw down the two wet black sticks and ran off. There wasn't much time left to play before supper.

The two sticks lay on the snow like a broken promise.

The next morning as I looked absently from the window, I noticed that the two sticks I had stared at so long the evening before were gone. I knew they were too big for birds to take. Maybe the kids had used them later for some other game. But I bet they swam away like two sardines, laughing.

Now it is spring and the kids want a kite. And I am feeling, in spite of these reflections, my annual urge to buy a can of sardines. Whoever invented that famous saying, "They never learn," was a pretty smart fellow. He probably also invented the kite, canned sardines and the Boy Scouts of America.

# FIGULUS AMAT IDAIAM

Primigenia must have been something. She lived in Nuceria, a suburb of Pompeii, about 2,000 years ago. No manuscripts were ever found in the ruins of Pompeii, but the graffiti scratched in the walls survive.

If it were not for the abundant graffiti about her, she would be an unknown. We even know from the graffiti that she hung out near the Roman Gate and that she lived on Venus Street. A lot of time has passed, but Cornelius, Secondus, Sabinus and Hermeros --those who included their names in their graffiti-- would probably not find it odd at all that people are still talking about Primigenia.

I don't think that Hermeros actually knew Primigenia because his long graffito contains a formal greeting to her, followed by an invitation. He was anxious to meet her: "Come to Puteoli and in the Timian street at the place of the baker Messius ask for Hermeros, freedman of Phoebus."

Not all Pompeian graffiti were as long-winded as that. Around the city was plenty of the familiar terse stuff: "Figulus amat Idaiam" (Figulus loves Ida); "Serena Isidorum fastidit" (Serena hates Isadore). Times have not changed.

At one school where I taught, they painted the stalls in the lavatories Bic Blue in an attempt to stamp out graffiti. A trick like that works in some schools, but a similar ploy failed at one local college when the students --maybe their professors, too-- took to writing in minuscule on the white latex grouting between the wall tiles. It's hard to out-fox the educated. The walls looked like some sort of inverse crossword puzzle where you were supposed to fill in the lines instead of the boxes.

At my present school, some of the kids are fond of using butane cigarette lighters to burn messages on lavatory ceilings. Each letter takes about a dozen torchings and the result resembles a petrified smoke signal. They seem to work in these dens with the diligence of the primitives who worked on the ceilings of their caves. Every man must make his mark.

I first learned about graffiti when I was a kid and my father hauled me up the front street to the corner where a few new slabs in the concrete sidewalk had just been poured. He pointed to my name which was scratched in the fresh concrete. I had not done it, but he was not quick to believe me because there was no one else in the neighborhood with that name --a fact he mentioned a few times. With the tip of his shoe, he began scraping at the name and he had it almost smudged over when a man came around the corner and gave him hell for defacing the new section of sidewalk.

The only one who left feeling innocent, I think, was the man who came around the corner.

I never learned who wrote my name on the sidewalk, but about five years ago, he resurfaced and wrote my name on the sides of two overpasses on Route 1 near Milford, Delaware. My name was still there last summer when I last passed through. According to the writing on the bridges, I love Stacey. But I have never known anyone named Stacey. I can't explain it. Maybe there is another me that I don't know about. If so, I hope that Stacey and I had a good time at the prom and I apologize to Milford for writing on the bridges.

A graffito showed up last month on the side of the Bradshaw road overpass on Interstate 95 just south of the Harford County line: "I love you Bonnie, Merle."

It attracts attention because you wonder how Merle got out there on the side of the bridge and because the overpasses on the highway were just painted and the paint jobs were in pristine shape until Bonnie and Merle came along.

There is a rumor spreading among commuters, who have no choice but to speculate about Bonnie and Merle once a day, that the message was written to Bonnie Raitt from Merle Haggard. Some are betting that the time will come when the Bradshaw Road overpass will be removed, taken to Nashville and put in a glass box at the Country Music Hall of Fame.

I can't help wishing well to Merle and Bonnie and to Carl and Stacey even though I find graffiti a social blight. Although we have come a long way from the days of Pompeii, our attraction to graffiti remains unchanged.

It even makes you wonder what the astronauts have written on the moon.

# SPEAK OF BABYLON

Frank Ashe was buried alive in the dump behind Harford Mall in Harford County in 1973.

Because of that I would like to see a memorial of some sort when the dump is closed and covered over.

Frank Ashe resigned his teaching position and went West when his wife died. He went to where there was desert and where the rising sun made shadows that were miles long. He wanted to live where he could catch sight of the almost-extinct American wolf, the prairie shark.

Frank Ashe ended up being buried alive in the dump behind Harford Mall when I got disgusted with how the novel was going and committed the manuscript to the dump. Ever since that rash moment, I have wanted those hundreds of typewritten pages back. I know that gasses and the pasty red mud have consumed it all by now.

What I have not wanted back from the landfill behind the mall are the pages of another manuscript, a get-rich-quick project that was going to be the ultimate sex-and-violence novel.

There is good money in sex and violence and I planned on making a fortune. But I overdid it. The story was so sexy and violent that all the women were pregnant and all the men were dead by the end of the first chapter.

It makes me wonder how many drafts of stories and novels have been sent by other residents of Harford County to the dump behind the shopping mall. It would be great if somehow the discarded manuscripts from all the writers could be recovered and excerpts from each published in an anthology of landfill literature.

I wonder, too, how many oil paintings and water-color pictures are pressed among the broken things there. How many reams of sheet music with penciled notations and eraser marks were finished off with a full-page X and dumped? From others there are tons and tons of letters, postcards, horrible telegrams.

A landfill is the macabre repository of personal history and of those attempts at creative things we use to fight for life, as well as the pit for the pieces of roof blown apart by storms, the stripped bones that link us to the animals, the bottles that held a million gallons of whiskey to ease the pain.

"Babylon once had 2 million people in it, and all we know about 'em is the names of the kings and some wheat contracts."

That line from Thornton Wilder's *Our Town* is part of a long folksy speech that supports the general theme of the play that our lives are at once both significant and insignificant. The popular play has been performed since 1939 by countless church and school theater groups.

In Grover's Corners, New Hampshire, were the play is set, the people were assembling things to be put inside the cornerstone of the new bank as a sort of time capsule.

They were including the local newspaper, a Bible, the Constitution of the United States and a copy of Shakespeare's plays. All the pages were going to be painted with "silicate glue" which would preserve them for a thousand years, maybe more.

The fellow in the play who speaks of vanished Babylon finds not only the silicate glue but the very contents of the time capsule laughable. He tells the audience that he is going to add a copy of the play they are watching because it is about the milk-horse routines of small-town life and the natural passage of simple people growing up, getting married and dying.

"Our Town" would be put inside the cornerstone of the new bank, according the stage character, so that the people of the future would "know a few simple things about us --more than the Treaty of Versailles and the Lindbergh flight."

I have come to think of the landfill behind the shopping mall as a sort of time capsule containing in a strange but very real way the story of "My Town."

I will let go my request for a monument to Frank Ashe who was known only to my wife and me. When the time comes for the people of the county to argue about what to put on top of the garbage, I will vote that a silence be allowed to hover above it.

# CHANGING PLACES

An anole, a small lizard that looks like a little brown rubber dinosaur, sits on the arm of the chair across the table from me on the lanai. I have been here long enough that I don't care what lizards do anymore.

Then the bottoms of the clouds take all the complex colors of peach skins. There is a period of very strong pink light. The water burns. Finally, a barn-red sun rises from the Gulf of Mexico. It is even hot at sunrise.

The people who usually live here have gone North to vacation in the mountains, but they have left themselves silently behind.

The great-grandfather's crab traps hang neatly on a wall in the garage over a work bench heavy with rusty medieval-looking tools brought from the shed on Roast Meat Hill when they left Connecticut nine years ago. The great-grandmother's water color paintings and those of her friends hang neatly on every wall of the house.

A closet filled with dark wooden things was opened when I was looking for a typewriter, and the antique scent of their old Eighteenth-Century house in the Connecticut woods flowed into the white and yellow of their modern Florida living room.

Everything is neat and in its place, including the cache of Connecticut air that came when they changed places.

Cervantes once unwisely observed that you could "journey all over the universe in a map." If that were so, I would only know that roads are red or blue and cities are yellow.

"I have never been in America; therefore I am free from the delusion commonly entertained by the people who have been born there, that they know all about it," wrote Bernard Shaw in 1928 when faulting the tendency of Americans to describe their country in terms of where they live, the square mile they know.

Changing places broadens understanding. I know I learned a lot about America just from the drive from Maryland to Florida on Interstate 95.

For instance, the population of North Carolina is nine.

They are all teenagers. Seven support themselves by running a McDonald's and two operate a gas station.

The population of South Carolina is four and they run a Stuckey's. From what I could see from the highway, no one lives in Georgia.

Florida, though, is densely populated and in the throes of a revival of utopianism. Most of the people here live in alternative realities: Disney World, Sea World, Circus World, Busch Gardens.

I could make a killing here building a park called Real World. Animals dressed in people costumes would roam the park and shake hands with little children. "This is the way it used to be," parents would say to their kids.

It wouldn't cost anything to get into Real World. But local teenagers dressed like muggers in colorful street-gang jackets would stalk the place and collect what they could. People who came to Real World could play games and win prizes like big stuffed orphan dolls and cans of spray paint they could take home and use to deface their neighborhoods.

We have met some real people in Florida.

Friends of the great-grandparents who live nearby invited us to lunch one day. They have a custom of pouring a new slab in an ever-growing path along the side of their house whenever guests come. We were surprised. Gin and tonic were mixed; so were concrete and sand.

As we knelt and wrote on our wet slab, they asked if we would include the name of our hometown, because that was where they last lived before they retired to Florida. They wanted proof for their Florida friends, they said, that there really was such a place.

As I scratched "Bel Air, Md." into the concrete with the tip of a stick, I thought of the closet full of Connecticut air just a few blocks away.

On evenings as lizards climb the screens on the lanai and mullet leap and splash loudly in the water-way at the end of the lawn, my wife and I have talked about where we might go when we retire. We have talked of snowy mountains, deserts out West, new ways of life.

It would be a shame to live and die in a square mile of Bel Air, Maryland. But it would take a lot of courage to get up and go leave it behind.

# NIGHT CROSSING

Strange things come on a dark wing.

Once there was a guy on the other side of a wall who used to beat his young wife at night. It went on for months until one night when the police came, they took him away and he didn't come back. I learned to distinguish the sound of furniture hitting the wall from the sound of the girl when she hit the wall. The neighbors took turns phoning the police.

The beatings never began when I was still awake. They would always start after I fell asleep. Thumping, crashing, muffled yelling would wake me. To wake suddenly in the midst of chaos is disorienting. Then I would realize that something horrible had been born and was thrashing against the wall. Then would come the rhythmic beating of the girl's head against the wall. I had learned the sound of her head.

I had learned, also, how to wake in dread at the sounds of innocent voices from the night. A starter motor on a car engine would grind away and I would find myself awake and hollow.

Often, for what seemed half a day sometimes, the youngest child on the other side of the wall could be seen standing on the sill of a closed window on the second floor with arms stretched out and up to hold her. Her body made an X across the window.

This picture from long ago that I had forgotten came back to me by surprise in a camera-quick flash the other night when I heard a cry in the darkness. I was standing on the porch with one of the children who couldn't fall asleep.

"What was that?"

"I don't know. It's probably teenagers walking around," I said as I pointed through the trees toward another street.

It didn't sound like teenagers to me.

I have found it convenient for the sake of the kids to blame happy-go-lucky teenagers for all noises in the night or anything strange that is found on the lawn in the morning. I may have to be careful about this because the kids are beginning to fear teenagers.

Everything was blamed on "hillbillies" by my mother when I was a kid. I know that I developed a fear of the hillbillies who would come every night to Baltimore from the Ozarks just to make noises under my bedroom window.

I never saw any of them, but I knew they were out there creeping around in long black beards and overalls held up with one strap.

A strange thing happened that night on the porch to a large tree in my neighbor's yard. It seemed that all the fireflies from all the yards had gathered in a tall oak near his house. For a few minutes, the tree twinkled like a Christmas tree. It happened suddenly and ended suddenly.

Another night there was a strange thing to hear. The train tracks are a good six miles away but we heard a train which we had not done in all the years we lived near the tracks. It was not a dull train noise. Each wheel click was fully distinct. There were metal screeches and creakings and what sounded like the jingling of chains. We listened in a tremendous hush as if something very important had come to pass.

I have taken a few walks by myself around the neighborhood on summer nights. In the darkness, a splashing sound from a stream that is piped under the street surprises me. Most of the post lamps at the ends of the driveways are lit and are too bright, too harsh. Squinting as I pass, I feel like I am under a light being questioned by police.

"What are you doing?" a post lamp says.

"I'm taking a walk."

Every sentinel-like lamp that is lit questions me as I pass. Some houses send out dogs to sniff me over.

Maybe my footsteps or the sound I make when I stop to rap my pipe against my shoe to empty it scares some little children who are going to bed. Their parents probably say, "It's a teenager" or "It's just a hillbilly" to comfort them.

Returning to my own house, I see the upstairs windows lit. The kids are being put to bed. The familiar voices sound different from this perspective.

Among the many bedtime books we have upstairs is *Good Night Richard Rabbit*, by Robert Kraus and the illustrator N.M. Bodecker. Richard says he can't sleep because he hears a giant, but his mother says it is only his father walking around downstairs. Richard says there are rocks in his bed, but his mother says his sheets need smoothing. It goes on like this until Richard says he hears a fire engine going by. His mother looks from the window and says, "So there is." Some things that happen in the night are imagined, and some are very real.

I look through my own windows with a stranger's curiosity. The darkness floods in around us like water.

# THE SHED RAISING

The shed monster appeared on the night when the lumber for our shed was delivered.

He is actually a large opossum, but he is called the shed monster by the kids because he often makes his entrance into our civil world from under the shed in our neighbor's yard. And there is a suspicion that he may live there, even though opossums are supposed to live in trees.

I think the shed monster came in the dark to sniff the lumber, plywood and bundles of shingles piled in the driveway. I was standing in the doorway looking out at all the building supplies that had been delivered that afternoon when the opossum walked slowly into the wedge of light that fell from the door. He prowled about a heap of pre-built barn-shaped trusses. Another shed for me to live under, he probably thought as he viewed the barn frames and gave to the project a shed monster's blessing.

I watched him and inhaled the scent of fresh lumber. I held a line of Arthur Miller in my thoughts that all a man needs is "a little lumber and some peace of mind."

But a little lumber is easier to come by than peace of mind. Knowing this, my wife did her best to clear the decks for me for a few weeks. She endured driving a car with a howling fan belt and doing laundry in the dark when the switch in the light fixture over the washing machine broke. She also mowed the lawn for me and did double duty in the area of little league game watching. Saturdays were roughest because she had to watch clinic baseball all morning and girl's softball all afternoon. I expressed my thanks by taking the 3-year-old off her hands and allowing him to be my helper. She thought it was a fair trade.

I then sort of hung out a sign that said Gone Shed Raising and walked away from it all into the woods out back where a place had been cleared.

Although I was working with only a mental blueprint and making up things as I went along, there was never any doubt about what I had to do next. For instance, if my helper was sitting on a concrete block, I knew it was time for me to set that block in place. How did I know where to set the block? Simple. Exactly where my helper was standing. When he walked off with the hammer, I knew it was time for me to hammer something. And the same was true for the saw, level and measuring tape.

If Thoreau had a 3-year-old in a red baseball cap to help him when he built his famed cabin in the woods at Walden, the history of American thought might be flowing a different course today.

Despite my helper, building the shed was not a chore for me. I worked with the relish with which Thoreau built his cabin. I hope that in the next life I will be assigned to building things in the woods. Which, I think, is not an unreasonable expectation for it does seem to be commonly supposed that paradise will be a grassy and wooded place.

Among the results of a recent national survey of Catholics was the finding that most people questioned envisioned heaven as a green park-like place. I am sure the visions of others would be the same if they were asked; a green heaven is an old conception of an after-world. The Greeks dreamed of the fields of Elysium and the Egyptians of Punt where cattle grazed under frankincense trees. King David sang in Psalm 23 of green pastures and still waters. The Eden of Genesis was an oasis, named significantly after Edin, the verdant plain of Babylonia. And paradise itself is actually a Persian term for a walled garden. Surely, there will be wells to dig and cabins to build there.

As I sat astride the ridge of the roof and drove the last nail into the last shingle, I cried, "Let it rain!" --as all true roofmen do, I believe, as they pound in the last nail. As if by magic, a storm that had been brewing all afternoon cut loose at once and lightning turned the sky flash-cube white as if in spark-like response to the last whack of the hammer against the nail.

The shed monster's blessing seemed to have been a powerful thing as it had not rained once during all the construction. My helper and I weathered the storm inside the shed. The two older kids envied him and came running out of the house and through the woods during the worst of the storm to join us. It was too dark and hot with the doors closed so we threw them open and let the wind blow the rain in on us.

I was a bit sad that the shed was finished, but the storm provided a distraction from such thoughts. Rivers of flood water ran through the yard and thunder cracked overhead as we speculated about what might come to live under our shed. The kids want rabbits, but now that the project is out of my hands, we will just have to wait and see what happens.

I'll settle for an opossum, even though they are supposed to live in trees.

# NEWS OF THE WIND MARKET

The bamboo chimes clatter like bones.

On some recent windy nights I have listened to the new wind chime hanging from a tree branch below the bedroom window. It was a gift sent from Japan by a friend of my wife. Because two wind chimes already hanging in the tree had been broken for some time, it was a welcome gift.

One of the silent chimes, a contrivance of bells and rods, had fallen victim to rust very quickly. And the other chime, made of shells, had thrashed itself to ruin shortly thereafter.

Hanging in a tree farther back in the yard is a heavy wooden wind screw which we got from a relative in California. The spiral is three-feet high, weighs many pounds and refuses to spin in anything less than a gale.

As I was hanging the new bamboo chimes, it occurred to me that with so many things hanging from trees in our yard (including strings of cranberries taken from the Christmas tree over a month ago and hung in the trees for the squirrels who refuse to eat them), a visitor might reasonably assume that we are Druids.

Listening to the wind is an old fascination.

King David, who ruled around 1000 B.C., hung the cithara that accompanied his psalms over his bed at night to hear the wind play the strings.

The Greeks, who built the marble Tower of the Winds on the Acropolis, hung wind harps just as we hang wind chimes. The wind harp is a soundbox fitted with tuned strings. As the wind god Aeolus breathed, the Aeolian harp played, the pitch and volume varying at the whim of the god.

Thoreau records an encounter with an American Aeolian harp in *A Week on the Concord and Merrimack.*

As he was walking at sunrise near the railroad in Plaistow, he heard at a distance "a faint music in the air like an Aeolian harp." He suspected that the sound came from the telegraph wire following the track. Placing an ear against a telegraph pole, he heard a soft humming "like the first lyre or shell heard on the sea-shore."

Thoreau observed that all things have "their higher and lower uses." The lower use of the telegraph wire was the transmission of information about the "price of cotton and flour." But in its higher use, the harp string of the telegraph wire "hinted at the price of the world itself."

In a somewhat comparable experience, I heard a fine wind chime on a bright autumn night at a marina on Galloway Creek off Middle River. Making tin-can clankings above, the wind knocked pulleys and lines against hollow aluminum masts on a hundred rocking sailboats. The deserted marina was a great wind chime.

Sailors hear it all the time and come to tune it out, my friend said. But for me, a visitor who had just received his first lesson in rigging the jib, it was a sort of second-class timeless moment as the air filled with a sound like pots and pans banging on New Year's Eve and the wind blew cold and free.

The wind was not always free, though.

Until the time of the French Revolution many peasants in Europe had to pay for the use of the wind.

It was near the end of the Twelfth Century when Pope Celestine III claimed the winds in the name of the Church and imposed a charge for their use.

This sounds silly at first, but the reason Celestine III attempted to corner the wind market was to suppress the development of the newfangled windmill (late in coming to Europe) and maintain the monopoly which tithe-paying landlords had on the grain-grinding business at their water mills.

The Church relinquished its claim to the wind in the Fourteenth Century, but for centuries thereafter landlords continued to charge for the use of the wind that blew over their lands.

If nuclear power ever "bombs out" and the current serious experimentation with wind-driven turbines accelerates, we may find a grand hullabaloo raised again over who owns the wind. And the price of wind, I think, will rise.

Now the wind blows free, unharnessed.

As I sleep I know that prayer wheels are spun by the wind in Tibet, that the bamboo sticks in my yard continue to clatter through the night, like an old-time telegraph, with news of the wind market and the price of the world.

# SUMMER SHADOWS

Brown moths at the back porch light make bat-like shadows.

From the porch, I see shadows of leaves from a car's headlights move on the wall of the house next door. It is the shadow of the crooked ornamental cherry tree out front. Between the houses the leaf shadows rush. They slide on the wall next door. There is a coming; a stillness, hanging; a sweeping away like foam on the surf.

I remember drinking beer from a quart bottle on the steps of a fraternity house on Calvert Street in Baltimore. A maple tree on the corner glowed in the streetlight as if it were high noon; the shadows of leaves were clear and sharp on the warm sidewalk. A cop pulled over a car full of transvestites for overloading the vehicle; nine in fancy dresses and beehive wigs; it was 1964. The cop ordered them out of the car. A wig fell off. We sat on the steps and watched the show, tilting quarts of Pabst as one fellow sat in the slant of shadow in the doorway and played the mandolin.

So much of youth is wrapped in shadows.

When I was a small child I slept a few times at my grandmother's house in the city. The lights from cars turning from Eastern Avenue onto Robinson Street made shadows of vague origin move on the ceiling of the front bedroom; from the street light, plants on the windowsill made on the opposite wall a jungle that climbed to the ceiling and, losing distinct shape at the fold in space, stretched broadly on the ceiling like a black canopy. From the window I could squint down the block to the bright intersection. It was a keyhole view of the city. People never seemed to stop crossing the street. Some people stood on the one corner I could see and laughed in the night.

In my bedroom in the suburbs there were no shadows. It was a bald new place with no trees. The red brick rowhouses burned under the summer sun. From the window of my bedroom there was always a distant hazy glow to be seen at night from a cluster of stores where Loch Raven Boulevard came to a dead end, at that time, at Joppa Road. During my teenage years I worked at a delicatessen under the hazy glow.

Saturday nights were slow. The old man would sit on his stool in the back of the store and polish his glasses over and over again on his apron; he would doze off, his shadow from the overhead light sitting crumpled like a paper bag at his feet. I would sit on my stool by the cash register up front, bitterly nurturing half-formed yearnings; when you are 16, you don't doze off. A car would slide up to the curb with its radio on; Rosie and the Originals singing "Angel Baby," perhaps. The girl would stay in the car; the guy in a white T-shirt would slam through the screen door and buy a pack of Luckies and two bottles of 7-Up. I would stand at the window and watch the car pull away, its headlights sweeping clear the way to love and freedom, letting shadows run and scatter wildly out of its way.

Two years later at Ocean City my friends and I tried our hand at picking up girls. We walked one night with a group of girls on the beach which was shadowy and moon-like. A square, squat guy took "picking up girls" literally, and picked up a girl and carried her playfully out into the water. But then he had a muscle spasm and dropped the girl into the ocean. Because his muscles were shaking, he couldn't help her and the girl nearly drowned. The girl was mad, choking, her clothes ruined; her girlfriends were horrified; they thought he had done it on purpose. The girls ran toward the boardwalk to get a cop or somebody's father. We ran off down the beach; the lights from an eerie tractor pulling a sand sweeper cast our shadows down the melon-rind curve of the sand for a distance that was probably infinite.

The other night, it rained just after I began skinning catfish on the back porch with a pair of pliers saved from the tool kit of a long-gone Volkswagen from my college days. One detached head, nerve-driven, gulped at the rain under the shadows of leaves that looked like lily pads. Through the sliding glass door I saw my wife --who thinks my new interest in fishing may have gone too far-- and the three children sitting on the sofa watching TV. I looked at them as if from a distance. The process by which I emerged from the shadows of youth seemed hard to figure out.

There is a fable by Aesop called "The Dog and His Shadow." A dog with a bone crosses a brook. He sees the shadow of the bone, reaches for it and loses the bone in his mouth. The moral has to do with the world being a tricky place.

# INTO THE LABYRINTH

Over the highway, above the whine of trucks running through gears in the mist, a flight of southbound birds unwound for a hundred yards into a perfect corkscrew of birds.

That was a morning sight.

For several evenings now, when the temperature drops suddenly and the sun slips just as quickly, a cat has been sitting on the roof of a car across the street.

It sits owl-like. Stiff. Perched above rolling shirt-colored waves of children playing in the street.

It faces west every evening where the sunset is obscured by trees. There is a monastic calm about the cat. It seems to see nothing.

One evening I put on a sweatshirt and wandered outside. The four-year-old found a long feather. It was a blue jay feather. He was excited.

"If you have a feather, you can fly!" he told me.

He held the feather extended from a hand and ran and flapped his arms. He was a primal creature.

I waited.

"It's not working," I finally said.

He stopped running and looked about.

"I need one for the other hand," he said.

He couldn't find one. He went to bed that night knowing that he was only a feather away from flying.

After dark, lately, the whole family has been watching a katydid which walks nightly on the sliding glass door to the back porch. In the porch light the katydid resembles a delicate snow-pea pod with six short flamingo-jointed legs.

It walks up and down the mirror of glass slowly, pausing often to lick an almost invisible foot. Unperceived by the katydid, we stand in the dark room and watch from the black side of the glass.

The birds, the cat, the katydid go about their curious business in a season of change. We are left to study and twist the myriad facets of life as if it were a Rubik's cube.

We keep a sharp eye on things and we are organized.

For instance, when an ice block the size of a bushel basket fell from the sky quite recently and landed in a yard in Perryman in northeastern Harford County, things began to jump on the Chicken Little hotline:

Telephones rang at the Scientific Event Alert Network, the Smithsonian Institution, the National Aeronautics and Space Administration, the National Oceanographic and Atmospheric Center, the Federal Aviation Administration, the National Weather Service, the Harford County Health Department, Aberdeen Proving Ground. The local newspaper reported all this at length.

But it was the eventual conclusion of all the king's horses and all the king's men that the Great Perryman Ice Block Mystery was, indeed, a mystery.

"We don't shoot iceballs," an official at the proving ground told the local newspaper. The proving ground is usually suspected as the source of just about everything unusual that occurs in northeastern Harford County, and I am sure officials have compiled a long, possibly humorous, log of amazing things for which they have had to deny responsibility.

The residents of Perryman collected fragments of the ice block in jars for analysis, but they were told this was futile because the sample jars were not sterile. Testing would not only provide misleading information, I guess, about the ice block containing baffling traces of strawberry jam or pickling spices.

The mythic Daedalus, architect of the labyrinth built in Crete to imprison the Minotaur, was good at both making and solving puzzles. He was challenged once to pass a thread through the spiral maze of a complex shell.

Daedalus solved the problem by not solving the problem. He drilled a small hole in the central eye of the shell. Then he tied a thread to the leg of an ant. He sent the ant into the shell through the small hole. The ant walked through the shell and brought the thread out into the daylight at the large opening.

But no one has found an ant to walk through the maze of the ice-block mystery.

I, myself, think that the fall of the ice block will be followed soon by a deluge of gin and a six-foot olive. Scientists will probably talk for ages of the miraculous Cosmic Martini Spill.

In the evolution of thought, I suspect we are very much creatures who believe we are only a feather short of flying.

# CAT-COG

The book I'm checking now says that Samuel Johnson would eat tripe at a cookshop and wipe his greasy hands on a dog. But I had always thought that it was oysters that Dr. Johnson favored and that he wiped his hands on a cat.

I told the oyster-and-cat version of the anecdote during the year-long family debate over whether we should get a dog or a cat as a pet. I can't remember the context or the point I was making, but I am sure it had something to do with my low regard for cats.

My wife was raised in a cat family, but I came from a dog family that disliked cats. The battle line in our dog/cat debate was clearly drawn.

It was never clear why my family hated cats. Like so many other people, they just did.

Cat-hatred is a relatively recent development in the history of the domestic cat.

The Egyptians domesticated the cat about 4,000 years ago. Egypt was rich in grain and the mousing cat was a boon to farmers. Wealthy Egyptians tricked out their cats with earrings and jewels. The cat eventually achieved a venerable status in ancient Egypt because its nocturnal wanderings were believed to be guided by the moon and the love-goddess Pasht. Cats lived freely in the temples of Pasht and they were worshiped.

The Romans took the cat from northern Africa and brought it to Europe. In Rome it replaced the tame weasel as the household mouser.

But trouble lay ahead for the cat. It was the cat's past. The cat's link with Pasht and the pagan symbol of the moon, along with its European association with witchcraft and Satanism, brought the weight of the medieval church down on its back.

Late in the Fifteenth Century, Pope Innocent VIII, who was trying to stamp out witches and pagan symbols such as the moon, decreed a persecution of cats. For years, cats were tortured and burned in the name of Christianity.

But after the period of cat-persecution passed, a taint of irrational cat-hatred flowed on in the current of time.

The medieval Cat Wars may strike us as unthinkably unenlightened, but once Proctor & Gamble was under attack by some Christian elements because the company employs a drawing of the moon (considered by some to be cabalistic) as a trademark. Not many people are concerned with this. But it seems the lesson of history that after the moon, cats are next in line.

Which is just fine for cat-haters, I guess.

But I am not a cat-hater anymore.

The other night I bowed out of a round of the family's dog/cat debate to go to the 7-Eleven store. I came home with a loaf of bread and a cat.

Everyone was surprised. Even I was surprised.

The young cat had been "dumped" at the store that afternoon --a thing which happens frequently, according to the cashier who had fed the abandoned cat and looked after it.

At the store I had stood and watched the cat for some time. It ran out to greet each car that pulled into the parking lot from the dark highway. Then it would return.

I sensed that among the turning gears of the universe, a watch-fine cat-cog with my name on it had slipped into place.

Actually, my wife was more appalled than surprised. She had wanted a "new" cat and not a "used" cat. She had imagined going to a pet shop, selecting a kitten, and getting some sort of papers. (It is a strange world, I think, where animals have papers and people don't).

But now she likes the cat, although I received an I-told-you-so look in the examining room when the vet said that the cat had ear mites. The kids like the cat, too. They were at the point where they would have settled for anything with four legs and a tail.

And the cat seems very happy with us. She will have to learn on her own how to deal with the chattering squirrels that cling to the sides of the bare winter trees in the yard. But I think she senses from the looks of us that we will protect her from born-again Christians and oysters.

# DEATH INCIDENTAL

Deceived by clear sky mirrored in the faculty room's large windows, a bird flew into the glass on a bright day and fell onto a projecting roof below.

I went to the window and found the bird directly under my gaze, its head down, wings spread. The winter wind shook the brown down flecked with yellow wisps on its back. The bird was breathing heavily. Then the head raised, paused and dropped leadenly.

But the bird was not dead. After a few moments of stillness, although the head never raised, heavy breathing began again.

In "Travelling through the Dark," poet William Stafford describes his discovery at night of a dead deer on a narrow road above a canyon. It had been struck by a car, not an uncommon occurrence in that place, and it was the custom for the safety of motorists to roll injured deer off the road into the river.

As the poet dragged the stiff deer to the edge of the canyon, he discovered that its side was large and warm: "... her fawn lay there waiting, alive, still, never to be born."

Before he pushed the deer into the river, the poet "hestitated."

Balanced against the hesitation in the darkness were forward-reaching headlights and the steady engine of the car.

People who drive country roads understand what Mr. Stafford means by "hesitation." And, perhaps, there are those who do not.

One night I encountered an injured deer blocking a lane on Cromwell Bridge Road. One leg was kicking. It happened on my return hours later that I was directly behind the county truck that had come to haul the deer away. For several miles the deer's head looked straight at me, its night eyes glowing piercingly in my headlights.

Another night, on Harford Road where it narrows to two lanes and twists north into the country, my headlights suddenly disclosed a column of mutt pups paused in a curve. The mother at the head was looking back. Then she turned and led the column forward. I understood shortly the pausing of the pack when I discovered a dead pup on the road.

On the same road one afternoon, I saw a beagle on its back, all four legs clawing the air. My hesitation was a tap of the brakes, then I had to accelerate strongly to keep the cars behind from driving over me.

These images came to mind as I watched the bird, which still breathed heavily with its head bent. I tapped the window with the handle of my coffee cup, but it did not respond.

I felt an odd sense of shame that I didn't know what kind of bird it was. On a scrap of paper I jotted a description of the bird.

Within 15 minutes the bird's rate of breathing diminished. The head had raised a little but the wings were still spread. I tapped on the window again, this time detecting a slight twitch of attention in the bird's head.

In another 15 minutes I discovered that the bird had closed its wings and its breathing appeared normal. Its head was up but still. Minutes later, the bird's head was moving alertly.

When I returned after an hour, the bird was gone. Later I checked a field guide without success to identify the bird.

Although the bird had survived, I was still troubled by a sense of inadequacy.

On a morning once, our country cats dragged a rabbit onto the back porch. It was not their first rabbit. Most of its fur had been torn out, and although it was a red mass, it was still breathing. Its eyes followed me when I came to drive the proud cats away. I imagined its night of terror at the claws and teeth of the cats.

I scooped the rabbit into a fishing net, carried it into the muddy woods, and hid it under damp leaves in a thicket. I knew I was not doing the right thing.

Or was I?

I felt limited by blood, mud, a good suit and leather shoes, and the fact that I was already late for school. I stood awhile before I left.

It is regrettable that often the best we can do is hesitate, and that the import of the pause is so unclear.

# BY THE DELPHIC HOLE

In the afternoon grass the striped cat luxuriates shadily.

Ordinarily, the striped cat and the two darks cats guard the yard silently from posts at the porch corners, but it is Sunday and the cats seem to have the day off.

The two dark cats sleep in the house; the smaller, having been out all night, which it seldom does because of its size, has been asleep all day in its towel-lined carton in the basement as a precaution, I imagine, against missing this evening's cat roundup and the secure sound of the closing of the basement door.

The larger dark cat, not known for ferocity though looking like a bear, sleeps on a granny-knitted afghan that cats are not allowed to sleep on. I see him as I pass and let him sleep in Sunday quiet.

Though not the bravest of the three, the large dark cat is clever and often uses his paws like hands. He will sit and with a paw lift chow from a bowl and deposit it in the water dish; after it soaks a while, he lifts the wet chow out of the water with a paw and raises it to a slightly bowed head to eat.

He is also master of the Paw Trick. When the other cats gently nuzzle each other for dominance at the food bowl, he sits on the periphery waiting for the right moment to extend a paw among the noses and pull the bowl away. While the other cats seem to discuss what happened to the bowl -- having never learned after thousands of Paw Tricks-- the large dark cat gets his licks in peace.

Now, instead of being on guard against birds, squirrels, mice, moles, two cats are asleep and one is stretching in the grass by the Tree Where the Dove Was and the Delphic Hole.

In the Tree Where the Dove Was is still a small, flat nest with two unbroken, but certainly lifeless, eggs. A dove had built a nest in cold weather when the cats tend to sit about the house, only to find in the first warm days that the tree was by a cat's post at a porch pillar. And the height of the nest was pitifully low, just slightly higher than the porch deck. The cats never climbed the spruce. Instead, they stared and stared until, after several days of nervous comings and goings, the dove flew away from the eggs and never returned.

The nearby Delphic Hole is a water-worn hole from a leak in a shallow sump line. A bit of mysterious white bone of plastic pipe can be seen. When the sump pump in the basement runs, the hole hisses and gurgles and the cats gather without fail when they are in the yard. They circle what seems an oracle's cave and listen intently.

By the Delphic Hole I sit in the grass with the striped cat who stretches and rolls languorously in the damp grass. It proffers its belly for scratching and does not push the hand away with the rear paws as usual. I look about and listen. No birds or squirrels seem about. I pull my hand away and the cat pulls at a finger with its paws, the claws not even extracted slightly.

Then the cat turns over and freezes, pulling its rear legs under into pouncing readiness. A squirrel is on a low branch farther back in the yard in the woods. But I see no familiar sign of hard-muscled, earth-hugging readiness. Instead, the cat rises slowly and ambles in a weary manner into the woods to the base of a tree and looks up.

The squirrel does not seem to have its heart in this encounter either. It makes no challenge. The cat springs lazily up the tree a little and holds on. The squirrel pauses, then passes easily away among the branches. The cat drops from the tree, returning without sniffing unusual twigs or curious grass blades and sits again by me.

It rolls and stretches as before until the sump line hisses. The cat stops and listens, then twitches upright, walks a few steps to the Delphic Hole and sits at attention. Without raising myself, I slide over to the hole to watch and listen with the cat. The cat looks at me quizzically, then turns its head back to the sounds.

The cat does not understand the forward hiss and, after the pump is off, the long wet glugging and wash as the pipe drains by drawing air through the leak at the hole. But it does not keep me from feeling, as I sit with the cat, like an infidel.

# ENDPAPERS

# Of a Piece

Like a box of doughnuts or shredded wheat, the work of Carl Pohlner seemed destined, in the early eighties, first for the dining room, then for the dump. Appearing in the morning edition of the Baltimore Sun, his writing was read by Marylanders over second cups of coffee or during the morning commute. By late afternoon, the smiles and the *Sun* were gone. Still, in the archives on Calvert Street the file marked "Pohlner" began to grow. Carl collected his columns, and at Loyola College, a cadre of admirers in the Writing and Media Department clipped and exchanged his articles to use as models in class.

Models of what? Certainly not of academic analytic work, but not of newswriting or editorial comments either. His articles are not poems, not short stories, not very short stories. They are not even essays though, like the essay, they are nonfiction prose literature. Generically at sea, most readers refer to columns that appear on the "op(posite)-ed(itorial)" pages of major newspapers as "pieces," a term that may do them more justice than the literati think.

"Piece" does not seem like much of a name for serious creative work. A "piece" of music, a "piece" of art, a "piece" of writing sound less substantive than a "sonata," a "watercolor," a "poem." The terms *poem, essay, story, novel* attach to genres with recognizable conventions and constraints. The thing that each is is definable; each has a name. "Piece" seems as multipurpose as sugar or salt. Refer to that block of words that occupies space on a particular newspaper page as "piece"? As easily call a rose not a rose but a portion or hazelnut coffee a sip.

Pieces of anything are in limbo. Puzzles wait to be assembled; cloth and cakes wait to be cut. "Pieces" anticipate or antedate action to which they inevitably submit. To refer to a Pohlner "piece" is oddly oblique. It asks what the writing once was and what it next will be.

Like any autocrat of the breakfast table, cutting his toast and spooning up jelly, not jam, Carl Pohlner's aim, in part, *is* to section, to select. In and about Bel Air and Baltimore, he leads an ordinary life that comes too fast, grows too familiar. A loving husband and father and son, he teaches school, swims in pools, commutes, computes, dries tears, baits hooks on piers, shops for socks, stops at the 7-Eleven, goes dancing, to the ballgame, the zoo, his in-laws', Florida, on endless errands. He sleeps and doesn't sleep, remembers being young, regrets growing old. Like all born-in-Baltimoreans, he likes crabs and hot dogs and harmonicas and beer. He finds Lite beer disturbing and light anything else. For a generation tired of microwave pancakes and dinner McMush, he stirs up life, looking for raisins or lumps.

His style is not slick and smooth. Short, quirky paragraphs bounce down the page. Boxed in black and white, his words color experience in wild and wondrous ways. He may wield a sword called "I've Seen It All Before," but, as he writes and we read, he and we see things anew. If his sky is not quite "a panoply of prismatic pizzazz," still, in ice cream stores, "the fluorescent lights even make the air look white," and stars shine in skies and on ties and in the roller rink where, under starbursts of colored light, Mr. Speed circles, his suitcoat turning purple and his eyes pink.

He upends expectation. His first published piece, "Mr. Rabbit and the Best Tradition," was written when his children and he planted a tomato and a rabbit appeared. "In a single stroke," he marvels, "my world turned upside-down." Cheerfully disconcerted, he browses for records whose theme is "I Won't be Home for Christmas," and he stares at double fir trees in glasses where shining eyes should be. "We were a noise the neighborhood would hear in the night," he says in "Night of Waking," where his penchant for reversal is clear: What we conventionally regard as the most important part of giving birth is relegated to parentheses: "(It was a boy)."

Like a barefoot boy walking a sandy beach, turning over shells and pebbles, he breaks the monotony of life in the last part of the twentieth century by picking out bits and pieces, musing over each odd shape, its muted colors flecked with pits and scratches and translucent streaks of light.

When he reads his work aloud, as he has done many times at Loyola College, Carl Pohlner seems young and boyish, full of chuckles, rather shy. Yet, he is not a boy, and although his work is grounded in his experience and one can piece together the life of Carl Pohlner from his collected works, neither biography nor boyhood reminiscence is the point. As he undoes his days, as he deconstructs, with as much fascination as someone confronting a puzzle, mosaic tiles, a trail of pawprints, or a game of chess, he also reconstructs, seeking pattern or design. He, on occasion, shrugs and says, "There's no deep meaning...Wonder simply exists --like a balloon on a string." Still, unstructured and spontaneous though his pieces seem, in their titles rests their intent: "Keeping Track," "Bearings," "A Handle on Things," "The Right Direction," "One Tangle at a Time," "Stumped" --all underscore that he not only makes pieces, but of his pieces something makes.

"In the bubble that comes from my mouth and sits over my head," he confessed in his tale of Mr. Rabbit, "there was a big black question mark." In the ninety-five pieces that followed, he struggled to resolve those questions --with considerable success. In "Finding Out," when a young high school graduate asked that he "tell us" some of life's secrets,

> I thought for a moment and then I did. I said that most
> of the good you find in life comes from self-sacrifice; that
> you have to develop a view of life that can accommodate
> loss and sorrow; that true love is hard work; that the
> most beautiful things in life come mostly in moments as
> small as a grain of sand.

In each piece that he writes, Carl Pohlner asks and answers, puzzling odd moments in daily life out. *A Feather Short of Flying* is a book of revelations compiled by a man in his middle years who has never recovered from a college philosophy course in which the carpet of complacency was pulled out from under his keds.

If the end of his work is philosophy, the means are decidedly not. His pieces are not logically reasoned. They are neither general nor abstract. Yet, to those moments of wonder that comes his way he has developed a genuine rhetoric of response. There are strategies whereby his particularized prose yields truths that stir, tug, and finally float free.

Anything, of course, set in type and titled gains credibility. Most of Pohlner's pieces were illustrated by Amy Salganik, whose Peanuts-like drawings promised Schulz-like scope. But within the prose itself is an actual grammar of pronouncement that brings things to a point. Many pieces have sentences of sheer certainty, as boldly stated as those in "Finding Out": "What really counts never changes"; "We have to keep reminding ourselves how good we really have it"; "The one advantage primitive man had over modern man, I think, was that he knew an omen when he saw one"; "Every man must make his mark."

More powerful than slogans are sentences whose sound seems to sanction sense. He trusts the promise implicit in poetry, that language (assonance, alliteration, metaphor, repetition, balance) by itself authenticates: "Youth is as dark as it is bright" or "White collar workers often have blue collar dreams" --we believe those sentences long before we see what they mean. In "a world full of dangles and unequatable things," Carl Pohlner recognizes the power of cadence alone to impose order: "And as I lamely cruised the boardwalk that night in my lone flip"; or "The white tee shirt was what was left when the blue collar came off at the end of a hot day."

In "The Big Two-Hearted Percolator," he laughs at what he calls "hemingwaying." To "hemingway," he tells us, "is to speak of something ordinary, like making coffee, as if it were quite meaningful." But everyday acts, like making coffee or cocoa or biscuits or music or money, *are* rich in significance--or might be. Language is one way to discover significance. Another is to bring to bear on the present the repository of the past.

As though truth grew through accretion, Carl Pohlner's pieces are layered with allusion. Full-fledged comparisons abound. With allusive word choice, he more subtly fuses present to past. When a wedding is referred to as "nuptials" and family as "diviners of signs" or "soothsayers," both humor and possibility result. With a lexical locus, he invokes, in "Walden's Other Chapter," the wild west: "I made another adjustment to the *lariat* knot in the length of clothesline...Birds aside, I was trying to *lasso* the top of the tree with the plan of *catching* it and *pulling the supple upper part* of it toward me... *Hoppy and Cisco* would not have been impressed... *A painted toucan* and *an armadillo of red clay shot* along the *waxed wood*."

His own and our shared pasts are to him pertinent and personable. He makes reference to almost every writer he has ever read: Twain, Swift, Keats,

Jeffers, Stevenson, St. Exupery, Salinger, Rilke, William Stafford, Shakespeare, Dickens, Hawthorne, Whitman, Arthur Miller, Frost, Orwell, Charles Lamb, Cervantes, Shaw, Wallace Stevens, Steinbeck, Jack London, even Mr. Hemingway, and, of course, Thoreau. A frequent visitor to the library in Bel Air, his references include paintings, music ("Hello Mary Lou!"), culture, pop culture, facts, famous figures (St. Valentine, Andrew Jackson, Louis XIV), foreign places. There are endless references to children's literature and to myth, folklore, legend, the Bible, fable. When references and parallel fail, he uses capital letters to give his experiences mythic proportion: "the ancient and intricate Cheese Trick," the "Hurried Parent," "the Feast of the Falling Ball," "the Paw Trick," "the Day of the Ice Skating Goose."

In pursuit of pattern, his writing reassembles bits and pieces drawn from the washed-up layers of time and space that man remembers and records. At the core is the oldest layer of all, the natural earth. Urban and then suburban, Carl Pohlner, too, dreams of earth. A transcendentalist at heart, his regret at man's removal from nature runs deep. As Baltimore encroaches on Bel Air, as the stars fade and the earth grows as synthetic as a styrofoam ball, he clings to what of the real remains. On a field trip downtown, he recalls, "at the library we left behind a constellation of noseprints on the locked glass door to the Poe Room. As I stood back, I thought it was a wonderful sight. I studied the stars on the glass and felt an intimation of a sense of direction in my new world." Into the new world he folds the old --stone fences, brambles and weeds, turtles he sprays with a hose until in "a fog-fine primeval mist, the turtles slowly emerged from their shells. In this ancient aura, they stretched their necks and looked about alertly." He spends a lot of time in his backyard where "the bamboo chimes clatter like bones." He longs to believe that the hiss of a sump pump and a "white bone of plastic pipe" somehow emanate from a Delphic hole, that the earth is more than we know, that age does not undercut awe.

Carl Pohlner is not overtly pensive. When he reads his work aloud, audiences laugh. But when I read a piece in the quiet of a sunny kitchen after everyone else in my family has gone, I find him a writer who does and does not take things lightly. "This goodly frame, the earth, seems to me a sterile promontory," mocked Hamlet. "What a piece of work is a man!" In each piece of work that he produces, Pohlner staves off an emptiness that from earliest time has led man, like Peter Pan, to sew lost shadows back to his feet. "Darkness and mystery are no longer a part of my clockwork and fluorescent life," he wrote in one of his early pieces. "It is something I am too old ever to touch again. Even the reaching hand of memory comes back almost empty --with hardly a smudge on a finger to prove that all the darkness was true."

His work may be read at the breakfast table, but he writes in the dim panelled recesses of his basement under the light of a bare bulb. From a single incident, he sets out to run us a merry chase, but his endings always bring us full circle and, particularly in the final section of the book, "Deduced Reckoning," we find he has encircled a sobering truth. Though he can see, in retrospect, the components of each piece, where each comes from and how, having freely associated, they all come to fit is as much a mystery to their author as to anyone. He is, ten years after beginning, an experienced writer, but in the Jamesian sense of the word "experience":

> The power to guess the unseen from the seen, to trace the implications of things, to judge the whole piece by the pattern, the condition of feeling life in general so completely that you are well on your way to knowing any particular corner of it--this cluster of gifts may almost be said to constitute experience.

What to call writing that guesses, traces, judges, feels? Though some of the tales he tells are fictitious, they are not stories. Because they "essay" to find a point, they resemble essays, but, without the spine of discursive thought, they are not. In their construction, they work like poetry, but, of course, they are not poems.

But they fit into no clear journalistic tradition either. It was fortuitous that Carl Pohlner's local paper happened to be the *Sun*. On the editorial pages of major American newspapers --the *Atlanta Constitution*, the *Boston Globe*, the *Detroit Free Press*, the *Houston Chronicle*, the *Los Angeles Times*, the *Miami Herald*, the *Washington Post*-- space is given to the paper's editorial staff, syndicated columnists, and writers with credentials (elected officials, authors, professors, businessmen, corporate leaders, Henry Kissinger, the head of the World Bank). The *Chicago Tribune* runs occasional short casual pieces under the title "The Observer." Bill Tammeus publishes "Starbeams" in the *Kansas City Star*. The *Canada Globe and Mail* runs daily columns by Thomas Walkom and, on Mondays, news from Madronna Island ("spring is here!") in a feature called "Treasure Island" by Jean Haworth. The Cleveland *Plain Dealer*, the *Philadelphia Inquirer*, and the *New York Times* do entertain the work of local freelance writers, but usually on topical matters.

Both Baltimore *Sun* papers, by contrast, encourage what properly can be called "pieces." Such op/ed editors as Stephens Broening and Hal Piper of *The Sun* and Gwinn Owens and Mike Bowler of *The Evening Sun* have published a steady stream of work by Maryland writers that is informed by both fancy and fact. It is to Broening and Piper that considerable credit for Carl Pohlner's first book is due. "Try to be one of the people on whom nothing is lost," urged Henry James in *The Art of Fiction*. As things fall apart --and each day things do-- Carl Pohlner has been a writer piecing together rags, bottles, bones, fishing rods, eggplants, Brownie pins, a haircut, his classroom day, featherstitching each to each as one might piece together a quilt. Like muslin or chintz, like roads and tracts of wood and farmers' fields, his "pieces" have a definite length --two and one-half double-spaced typed pages. But his pieces are not set pieces. No two are alike. His vision is vocal, not visual, his work shaped by voice, his voice the legacy of an old oral tradition, of rocks or rockers around a fire, of back porches on hot summer evenings where friends and family celebrate the "gathering of darkness and forming of stillness."

Evoking that past, for young and old alike his work makes wonderful reading. In *The Human Comedy*, William Saroyan writes, "The pattern of life in Ithaca --of people everywhere in the world-- followed a design which at first seemed senseless and crazy, but as the days and nights gathered together as months and years, the pattern was seen to have had beauty of form." Carl Pohlner's work gives shape to a decade. As each piece whirs in the dead of night through the assembly-line production of the morning *Sun*, it remains the product of cottage industry. Handcrafted, it is paid as piecework, submitted, unsolicited, to its publisher, who then pays a set amount. The work is piecemeal, production per year rising and falling as mood and circumstance ebb and flow.

Carl Pohlner has not written a piece in 1989, but, as he is still a feather away from flying, as finding out is as long as your life, as days and nights still find him, in limbo, staring at his refrigerator or at stones or seashells or stars, surely he will write again. Perhaps he will write a piece about the piecing together of the pieces that make up his book. Neither he nor we can predict what such a piece might be --except, perhaps, for its very last line:

(It was a joy.)

Barbara Mallonee
February 1, 1989

*Barbara Mallonee is an assistant professor of writing at Loyola College in Maryland. Her "pieces" also appear on the opinion page of the Baltimore* Sun.

# LITERARY CHRONOGRAPHY

1979

| | | |
|---|---|---|
| 1. | Mr. Rabbit and the Best Tradition | June 13 |
| 2. | Bathtub Melons, Dancing Crabs | July 25 |
| 3. | Chicken in a Sweater | August 15 |
| 4. | Of Angels, and Pinheads* | August 16 |
| 5. | With Bright, Shining Faces | September 5 |
| 6. | Puppet Peril | September 27 |
| 7. | Night of Waking | October 16 |
| 8. | Ratatouille with Wallace Stevens | October 31 |
| 9. | The Hound of the Pohlnervilles | November 20 |
| 10. | Christmas on the Road | December 4 |
| 11. | A Case of Rampant Class | December 18 |

1980

| | | |
|---|---|---|
| 12. | Getting it Rite the First Time | January 8 |
| 13. | The Chain-saw Boys | January 24 |
| 14. | The Right Direction | February 6 |
| 15. | The Lure of the Gold Line | February 22 |
| 16. | Just a Little Heart | March 26 |
| 17. | Upstairs, Downstairs | April 15 |
| 18. | Frankenspeed on Urethane | April 29 |
| 19. | The M&M Future (not included) | May 16 |
| 20. | Thrills of the Real World | June 3 |
| 21. | On the Barrel Head | July 1 |
| 22. | The Return of Sherlock Holmes | July 31 |
| 23. | Frolicking* | August 23 |
| 24. | I've Seen It All Before | September 2 |
| 25. | Omens, Rain or Shine | September 26 |
| 26. | The Eyes of Plimoth | October 28 |
| 27. | Vaporized, Full Blast | November 21 |
| 28. | Unpacking Christmas | December 9 |

## 1981

| | | |
|---|---|---|
| 29. | Low Rolling | January 9 |
| 30. | Catcher in the Wheat | February 4 |
| 31. | It All Depends | February 19 |
| 32. | Out of Time and Space | March 3 |
| 33. | Why Green Beer | March 17 |
| 34. | Rags, Bottles and Bones | April 1 |
| 35. | Wire Work | May 6 |
| 36. | Penates and Crackerjacks | May 19 |
| 37. | The Black-Robed Wizards | June 9 |
| 38. | Those Quiet, Dim Summer Evenings | June 26 |
| 39. | Tea Myths | July 15 |
| 40. | The Big Two-Hearted Percolator | August 5 |
| 41. | The Royal Wedding of Sherlock Holmes | August 20 |
| 42. | One Tangle at a Time | September 4 |
| 43. | A Handle on Things | October 9 |
| 44. | A World of Unequatable Things | October 29 |
| 45. | I to I | November 19 |
| 46. | An Inch and Many Miles | December 22 |

## 1982

| | | |
|---|---|---|
| 47. | Dreaming of Earth | January 19 |
| 48. | Shear Horror | February 24 |
| 49. | Only the Beginning | March 16 |
| 50. | Promises, Promises | April 20 |
| 51. | Figulus Amat Idaiam | May 11 |
| 52. | Death in the Afternoon | June 1 |
| 53. | Speak of Babylon | June 29 |
| 54. | Playing the Game | July 16 |
| 55. | Changing Places | August 20 |
| 56. | Stepping Ahead | September 7 |
| 57. | Night Crossing | September 23 |
| 58. | Once Over Lightly | October 13 |
| 59. | Say it with a Crock | November 24 |

## 1983

| | | |
|---|---|---|
| 60. | Dull and Delightful (To Bed, to Bed) | January 6 |
| 61. | Oops (not included) | February 20 |
| 62. | Cosmic Levity | March 22 |
| 63. | Stumped | April 6 |
| 64. | Spice of Life | May 11 |
| 65. | The Shed Raising | July 5 |
| 66. | Guilt with Mustard | July 27 |
| 67. | Yard Turtles | September 20 |
| 68. | The Sting | November 2 |
| 69. | Bless Ye, Boxholder | December 8 |
| 70. | Bearings | December 22 |

1984

71. Keeping Track, (January 1984)    January 19
72. A One-Skyrocket Holiday    February 7
73. News of the Wind Market    February 21
74. Green Badge of Courage    March 12
75. Fish Story    May 1
76. Finding Out    June 5
77. Summer Shadows    July 4 & 17
78. Into the Labyrinth    October 19
79. Cat-Cog    November 28
80. Walden's Other Chapter    December 21

1985

81. The Teachernaut (not included)    January 17
82. Breathless    March 19
83. On Balance, Happiness    July 5
84. Suckling's Flight    August 6
85. Long Time Passing    September 26
86. Side by Side    November 26
87. Signs and Their Times    December 24
88. Driving the Wrong Way    December 31

1986

89. Pier Review    January 20
90. Starting an Orange    February 18
91. Owl Story    July 28
92. White T-Shirts    September 8
93. U-Haul Kids    November 5

1987

94. Death Incidental    February 2
95. By the Delphic Hole    June 23

1988

96. New Life (not included)    April 2

*Originally published in *The New York Times*.